A WAY OF LIVING

A WAY OF LIVING

The simple life and extraordinary craft
of landscape painter
DON KOESTNER

Bill Hakala

OBIRIS
BOOKS
AFTON, MN

Obiris Books

Requests for permission to make copies of any part of the work should be mailed to the following address: Obiris Books, P.O. Box 250, Afton, Minnesota 55001.

Library of Congress Cataloging-in-Publication Data
    Hakala, Bill
        A way of living: the simple life and extraordinary craft of landscape
        painter Don Koestner / Bill Hakala
        Hard cover edition ISBN 978-0-9773377-1-2
        Paperback edition ISBN 978-0-9773377-2-9
        Preassigned Control Number: 2008906935

Manufactured in the United States of America
Printed by Sexton Printing, St. Paul, MN
Bound by Midwest Editions, Minneapolis, MN
Copy Editor: Ellen Green, St. Paul, MN
Index Editor: Pat Green, Homer, AK

Book design and production: Victoria Hakala
Text typeset in Sabon, designed by Jan Tschichold in 1966/1967
Printed on 70 lb. Natural Cougar Vellum with photos on 80 lb. Centura Dull

Contents

Photo Section I follows page 40
Gallery of Landscape Paintings follows page 72
Photo Section II follows page 120

Preface

The poetic vision and technical mastery of impressionist painter Don Koestner is evident in the many hundreds of paintings he has produced over the past half century. His art mirrors his core abilities: drawing and composition; paint handling; faithful interpretation of color and values; and visual memory.

Less apparent on the canvas is the foundation of his art: his roots and early motivation; his resourcefulness and perseverance; and his practical skills and problem-solving ability. The authenticity of his paintings—their poetry, mood, and honesty—stem as much from the man as from his brush.

Readers of all ages and interests can draw inspiration and instruction from the consistency and fullness of Don Koestner's long and productive life. A lifelong conservationist, he lives what he preaches. He draws his water from the world's largest freshwater lake and heats it with the sun. By most measures he has lived *simply*, and this choice enabled his growth and achievement.

To Koestner, art is like walking and breathing—a natural response. He says, "I didn't find art; art found me."

The lyf so short, the craft so long to lerne.

Geoffrey Chaucer

Pen and ink drawing of Don Koestner by
Cliff Moen, 1948

*Art and Religion are not professions: they are not occupations
for which men can be paid. The artist and the saint do
what they have to do, not to make a living,
but in obedience to some mysterious necessity.*

Clive Howard Bell

Footings

IN LATE SEPTEMBER 2004, DON KOESTNER DROVE from Silver Bay, Minnesota, to Balltown, Iowa, nearly 400 miles. Eighty years of age, he allowed himself two days to drive each way—a 10-day painting trip. He spent five mornings developing one 12-by-22-inch oil sketch and several afternoons on another sketch nearby. He stood at a collapsible French easel designed for outdoor painters trekking to sites far from the road. Attached was an umbrella to block the sun from his canvas. Koestner's portable painting kit included a plumb line, black mirror, reducing glass, brushes, and 14 tubes of hand-ground oil colors plus a large tube of Old Holland Cremnitz white. He worked slowly and methodically, adding one layer of color at a time. "Painting is not a spectator sport," he once told an observer who requested a demonstration. And, "I am an emotional painter, not an idea painter."

In Koestner's gradual development as a landscape painter, "getting it right" always preceded painting what he felt or thought. First he blocked in the scene's basic pictorial elements—fields, woods, buildings, clouds—then deftly voiced his overall perception of the experience with line, color, and values. Authenticity was his benchmark. Not a wildlife illustrator's "show every feather" depiction, but a scene filtered through his sensibilities and trained eye at a moment in time. One painting might take him months or even years to complete.

Koestner has spent more than a half-century recording the natural world. His work reflects his fascination with light, his close observation of nature in all seasons, his technical knowledge of late-nineteenth-century landscape painting, and his reverence for the impressionist painters whose works inspire him. He is one of few oil painters still preparing his own canvases from raw linen and grinding his own pigments to achieve subtleties and intensities of color not obtainable with commercial paints.

He works with an artist's eye for beauty and harmony and a farmer's eye for weather. His craft demands a mastery of drawing, composition, and color; a reverent and receptive spirit; patience and diligence; stamina and focus; and a visual memory for fast-changing light in an outdoor—*plein-air*—environment that is never steady or predictable. His work also requires a backpacker's tolerance for gnats, mosquitoes, wind, sudden showers, and sometimes finger-numbing cold. He sees landscape painting as a calling more than a vocation: "Painting is who I am and what I do."

Simple living is the foundation of Koestner's development as a traditional landscape painter, for it has provided him the best means to achieve his goals. Following art school, he knew he needed a dozen or more years to acquire any mastery of his craft; he would also have to support himself on minimal sales while painting in a style that he recognized even then to be unpopular and "out of vogue."

Koestner's Thoreau-inspired decision in 1950 to adopt a bare-bones lifestyle came at a time when America was entering a post-war economic boom. Opportunities for "life-time employment," higher wages, company pensions and paid vacations, 30-year home mortgages, and easy credit gave many a way up the socio-economic ladder. Koestner chose the less-traveled path and took his chances. Optimism and luck were often his companions, but he wasn't foolhardy. Practical and disciplined, he kept himself unencumbered and free of debt. "In obedience to some mysterious necessity," he devoted his time and energy to developing his talent and doing what gave him the most pleasure in life. He followed his dream.

—⁓—

Don Koestner was born November 28, 1923, at Mounds Park Sanitarium, a general hospital on St. Paul's east side, not far from the tiny apartment his parents rented above a store at 1090½ Arcade Street. The fact that the Baptist hospital's many medical specialties included obstetrics and pediatrics was fortunate for the artist's parents, Jack and Frieda Koestner. At birth their son suffered convulsions so severe they thought he would not survive more than a day or two, and they quickly planned his baptism at the hospital. Jack and Frieda named the infant Donald. Frieda's mother suggested the middle name Edgardine—a name "out of nowhere." After Donald's baptism, the convulsions ceased. This prayed-for but unexpected outcome was the first of many lucky turns in Koestner's productive life, events he later ascribed to a "guardian angel" or "helping hands."

Don Koestner's paternal great-grandfather, Joseph Andrew Kestner, emigrated from Austria to Minnesota in the late 1880s and homesteaded in Sherburne County, near the town of Becker. German-speaking people constituted the largest foreign-born group in Minnesota from 1860 until 1905 when the Swedes took over. In an era of shifting European political alliances, "German" often applied to anyone speaking German primarily, including those living in Austria and other areas bordering Germany. Kestner and his wife, Margaret Haberl, brought to America five sons and a daughter.

The eldest son, John Andrew—the artist's grandfather—added an "o" to his last name to eliminate confusion with his brother, John George's, mail. He eventually settled in West St. Paul—a melting pot of immigrants. John Andrew worked downtown as a cigar maker. Two of his daughters, Florence and Margaret, also made cigars, but at their father's home on West Bernard Street. (The *St. Paul City Directory* for 1892 records 66 cigar manufacturers in the city; by the mid-1930s only nine remained. Photographs from the period show workers sitting at long tables in large rooms, rolling cigars from leaf tobacco.)

Don's father, John (Jack) William Koestner, was one of the cigar maker's seven children, his eldest son. Tall and broad-shouldered, Jack sometimes played guitar on weekends at local barn dances. While employed as a St. Paul streetcar conductor in 1918, he rescued a passenger from a mouse hiding near her feet. Borrowing her umbrella, he deftly eliminated the menace. Jack and the damsel in distress began dating and soon married.

Frieda Umbreit Koestner was born in Calgary, Alberta, Canada. She was a tiny woman with brown eyes and an oval face crowned with coarse black hair—so coarse, her daughter, Lorraine, remembered, that "sparks flew when she combed it." Jack called Frieda "my Bitsy." Although she lived a long life and kept a tidy house, she was somewhat frail and tended to stay in the background. She had a wry sense of humor and once described a scrimping neighbor as "buttering her toast so thinly that she ended up with more butter at the end of the week than she began with."

Frieda's father, Ernst H. O. Umbreit, was a German immigrant who had entered North America through Canada in 1894. A shoemaker by trade, he was given to wanderlust. One evening in 1917, he disappeared from their home in South St. Paul. He had removed every photograph of himself that he could find, and was never heard from again. Why Ernst left so abruptly was not known. According to an early Umbreit family chronicler, "Only he knew his goals, ambitions, and dreams." (A recent Umbreit family search discovered that Ernst had in fact resettled in St. Louis, Missouri, married a younger woman without disclosing that he was already married, and at the age of 49 began a second family. He sold insurance for a living and died in 1960 in Monroe County, Illinois, near St. Louis.)

Left to care for Ernst's eight abandoned children in South St. Paul was his German-born wife—Frieda's mother—Wilhelmina Pfaff Umbreit. Years later, while selling corsets door-to-door on St. Paul's Grand Avenue, Wilhelmina met Fred Olson, a Swedish immigrant and former coachman for railroad baron James J. Hill. Olson was a widower and Wilhelmina soon decided it was time to declare her husband Ernst either dead or missing. Wilhelmina and Fred then married and took up life together in Olson's small, handsomely furnished house between Lexington Avenue and Dunlap Street.

Don Koestner's extended family of uncles, aunts, and cousins were steady, earnest, and industrious people. For the most part, their conservative habits and actions did not reflect the flamboyance and extravagance of the Roaring Twenties into which Don was born. The times were colored by heroic events: Minnesota native Charles A. Lindbergh's solo flight across the Atlantic to Paris and Babe Ruth's 60 homeruns in a season.

In November 1923, America's economy was healthy and growing. The financial crash of 1929 that launched the Great Depression was still six years ahead and the *St. Paul Pioneer Press* offered comforting forecasts: "Business throughout the U.S. is on a sound constructive basis … production and consumption seem to be pretty well balanced." Men's two-trouser suits at the Golden Rule cost $40; women's shoes at Field Schlick & Company were $7; a Ford Model T Runabout cost $265 (excluding self-starter and demountable rims, for an additional $85). Sophie Tucker performed live at St. Paul's Palace Theater, and downtown movie theaters featured *Six Cylinder Love* and *The Covered Wagon*—both silent films. Prohibition laws didn't stem the flow of alcohol. In November, federal agents in St. Paul raided 12 illegal stills on Pig's Eye Island and at Swede Hollow, destroying 20,000 gallons of mash and 500 gallons of moonshine.

Until Don was 10 years of age, the Koestner family—including the artist's sister, Lorraine, born four years before him—lived in a series of rented apartments and rented homes in St. Paul, the last of them a duplex on Annapolis Street. Another family lived next door, a common wall separating the two. On either side and across the street were other two-family homes. The neighbors gathered on porches in the evening to talk—the men on one porch; women on another. The children chased around the houses and on the street, playing Kick the Can and Run Sheep Run. Just a few blocks from their home was Cherokee Park, a Mississippi River overlook offering views of downtown St. Paul.

Koestner was a good student at St. Paul's Sibley Grade School. Class photos reveal a boy with straight, dark hair and a ready smile—an eager, friendly face. His slight build, brown eyes, and dark features strongly resembled those of his mother. He demonstrated a talent for art early in his life. Lorraine remembers him "drawing cars on the cardboard separators that came in the Shredded Wheat box." His first-grade teacher once commented on a picture of a building he had sketched. She said to her smiling, left-handed student, "Don, that's a very good drawing." Then she added, "Maybe you'll be an artist someday." Perhaps the remark was offered casually, but he never forgot it. He had not thought about what he would become because "someday" seemed a long way off. Years later he said, "I didn't choose art as a vocation; art chose me."

Neither Jack nor Frieda found anything to encourage or boast about in their son's talent and interest; they considered art impractical—a waste of time. In the working-class world of his parents and relatives, Koestner said, "Art did not exist." He found one exception to that perspective in his Grandmother Wilhelmina, who once took him by streetcar to Minneapolis to visit the Walker Art Center.

Koestner's art interest lay deeper than either of his parents understood, and to him their disapproval was crushing as well as puzzling. Jack found his son's interest in art embarrassing, and he could not discuss it with friends and relatives. Koestner males were "working men"—people Jack regarded as practical and useful. In his view, men built houses and sidewalks, made bricks, assembled machinery, butchered hogs, hauled freight. They put in a good day's work and could be counted on to get the job done. Artists made pictures to decorate walls and sold them at street fairs or took them door to door. They worked only when they felt like it and seldom amounted to a hill of beans. Even worse, art was "fancy." Frieda agreed with her husband—or kept silent anyway.

"I was an enigma to my parents," Don Koestner said. "Like

somebody they had never known before."

Despite their differences, father and son shared an interest in auto-mechanics. Growing up, Koestner watched his father's big fingers tug and twist on fuel lines, carburetors, and spark plugs to bring a sputtering engine back to life. Jack demonstrated diagnostic skills and mechanical savvy that his observant son later put to good use.

Some of their father-son experiences tested their compatibility. Among them was deer hunting with Jack's weekend fishing and hunting partner, Hank Schmidt. Don enjoyed being in the woods, occasionally shooting a squirrel or rabbit with his .22 rifle on solitary outings, but he found little reward in harvesting wildlife. For him, deer hunting took all the fun out of being outdoors and he thought his father and his hunting pals went about it too seriously—"like a business." They usually assigned Don the role of crunching through underbrush to flush the animals toward the waiting sharpshooters. Sometimes Don feigned getting lost to separate himself from the hunting party and enjoy the woods.

Jack Koestner was for the most part amiable, good-natured, and well liked, but with an eighth-grade education he struggled to get ahead. He resented the educated people he saw as moving up while he stood still. The term "jack-of-all-trades" fit him well. He worked as a streetcar conductor, butcher, mechanic, brickyard laborer, and pressman. He sold life insurance briefly, but was more inclined to work with his hands. He also liked to garden, and later in life raised a special strain of strawberry that produced through the summer. Relatives and neighbors often turned to him for help with car repairs and home-improvement projects. He laid floors and hung wallpaper for relatives without charge.

Jack also had a knack for reading human behavior. On visiting his father-in-law, Fred Olson, who was unable to walk unassisted, Jack urged him to use his crutches. The old man refused, insisting that the crutches were too long. Jack felt sure the pre-scribed length was correct but took them to Olson's basement and with a saw made two loud cuts on a broomstick. The sawing noise convinced Olson that Jack had fixed the problem. After taking a few steps with the unrepaired crutches, Olson said the crutches were much better now and began using them.

Jack's longest employment was with Minneapolis-Moline Power Implement Company. There, he put his mechanical skills to use on the production line, assembling farm machinery and buses at the company's Lake Street plant. One day a bus wheel fell on his foot. He was hospitalized for 10 weeks when the injury became infected, causing the removal of two toes. He collected disability for several months and was then laid off. With the 1930s depression deepening, work became scarce. Jack earned $15 a week when employed (about 30 cents an hour for a 48-hour week) and paid $20 to $30 monthly rent. For a time, the Koest-ners owed back-rent on a succession of homes, but years later Jack and Frieda proudly declared they had paid back "every cent."

Eventually, Minneapolis-Moline called Jack back as a work safety coordinator. But he thought the drive to Minneapolis from St. Paul a waste of time and money. The family moved to Min-neapolis in 1934, renting a succession of houses until finally buy-ing one in 1941 on 39th Street and 40th Avenue South.

To Don, Minneapolis never felt as much like home as St. Paul where he had spent most of his first 10 years. Leaving friends behind, he entered a new school system where the teachers imme-diately raised concerns about his speech. He spoke with a slight slur and a rasping voice—as he'd always spoken and which seemed normal to him. Minneapolis school counselors recom-mended he spend two months at a summer speech camp in Michi-gan, where speech therapists could provide him help. To qualify for the camp—expenses covered by the Minneapolis school system—he first had to pass a series of tests designed to measure his cognitive abilities. With the exception of math, Koestner remembers getting high scores. His parents put the eleven-year-old on a train to Chicago. An aunt living there had her boyfriend meet the train and take Don to a restaurant before putting him on his next train to Traverse City on the eastern shore of Lake Michigan. It was the first time he spent a night away from home alone and he was "scared to death."

At Camp Shady Trails, a counselor took Don out in a rowboat every afternoon for an hour. While Don rowed to build his upper-body strength, the counselor read aloud adventure stories by the nineteenth-century British writer and explorer Richard Francis Burton. (At home, Don's sister Lorraine read to him because reading gave him headaches.)

Koestner had an hour or so of daily speech therapy to improve his enunciation, especially his Rs. An attempt to teach him to swim by throwing him into the lake caused him more panic than useful instruction. Although he enjoyed some aspects of the camp, he made few friends and came away from the experience feeling less confident than when he arrived. Before camp, he had never thought of himself as being different or handicapped in any way. Now he did.

In a follow-up letter to Jack and Frieda, the camp counselors recommended that Don exercise with a chin-up bar and continue speech therapy. Regarding the speech problem, Jack told his son, "You're lucky you can talk at all," referring to his near death from convulsions at birth. They couldn't afford therapy.

—‌‌ιιι—

A HIGHLIGHT OF DON KOESTNER'S SUMMERS as a city boy were occasional visits to his Uncle Frank's farm near Becker, in Sherburne County, north of the Twin Cities. This was the original family homestead, where his Grandfather Kestner had lived before moving to the city. The farm was worked jointly by Frank and his brother Andrew, a lifelong bachelor who lived nearby.

Uncle Frank was Jack's uncle and Don's great uncle, though he was just three years older than Jack. Frank, too, had added an "o" to his name to make it Koestner. His 40-acre parcel was one of thousands of the subsistence farms still common across America in the first half of the twentieth century. Most supported an independent, modest way of life. Farmers were attentive to their animals and crops, self-reliant, and conservation-minded. Don remembered his uncle as a kind, compassionate man, someone he admired for his "laid-back approach to life."

The Jack Koestner family often visited the farm on weekends to hunt or pick berries, and Don stayed there for a week or two several summers during the 1930s. Uncle Frank grew corn and hay as feed for his animals. Don was amazed at how little food was wasted. Pigs and chickens ate table scraps. After living nearly 45 years on the farm, Frank's garbage dump behind the house was no more than a small pile of rusting tin cans. He plowed with horses, hand-milked his cows, and harvested with a threshing machine pulled by a neighbor's steam-powered tractor. Neighbors got together to help each other at harvest time. Several of them also spent two weeks each summer working off their county tax bills by regrading local gravel roads with a team of horses and a mechanical scraper.

Don got the flavor of rural life on these summer visits. He walked through the pastures to bring in cows for milking. Frank's dog helped move the cows down the path to the farmyard. The first time Don took part in this daily ritual, he noted that the dog left two cows to graze. When he asked why the dog ignored them, Frank explained, "The dog knows those are your Uncle Andrew's cows."

Sunday was the only day of rest on the farm—except for milking. On Sunday afternoons, Uncle Frank, his son Frankie, and Don sat on the roof of the henhouse to crack the hazelnuts drying there and listen to Uncle Frank's droll stories. One that made them laugh was about a neighbor who jumped off a highway bridge into the Elk River, intent on drowning. "Turns out the water was only a foot deep," Frank said, "and so cold that once he got in it he changed his mind and walked back home."

Don's second cousin Frankie was just two years older, and the two had good times together. But when Frankie was 15 he died of acute mastoiditis, an ear infection treatable today with antibiotics. Don inherited Frankie's catalog-ordered Montgomery Ward bicycle—a bike with nonstandard 27-inch wheels, the tires for which were only available from the Montgomery Ward warehouse near University and Snelling Avenues in St. Paul. During the next several years, Koestner said, "I almost literally drove the wheels off that bicycle."

On summer days he rode his bike along streets following the Mississippi River bluff—"often going all day on a bottle of pop." He biked east across the Ford Parkway Bridge to St. Paul, then followed Mississippi Boulevard south to the Seventh Street Bridge—about three miles—then back again. The area was mostly wooded, with an occasional old shed or house, one of them rumored to be a former hideout for John Dillinger, the notorious gangster gunned down by federal agents in Chicago in 1934. Along the way, Don might stop to sketch a tree that caught his eye. Often he returned to a spot several times to complete his careful drawing. Although he learned basic perspective in his seventh-grade art class, he got his best information from a Watson-Guptil drawing book, *How to Draw Trees*. "The book even provided instruction on how to make a portable, waterproof drawing board," he said. Not one to discard anything useful—a life lesson from his Uncle Frank—Koestner still has the drawing board.

During this period, the Koestners lived about a mile from the Mississippi River's Ford Dam. The young artist's proximity to the river, combined with his shyness about drawing in public, helped him develop a good visual and factual memory. He later wrote:

"Paddle-wheel towboats had a distinctive whistle, and when one of them announced its entrance to the locks, I hopped on my bike and rode to a spot above it. There I observed and tried to remember the shapes and details of a particular boat, then biked home to do a pastel."

Koestner practiced the same technique while visiting his Uncle Frank's farm, where his art interest was no more understood or appreciated than at home. At night, he made drawings of farm animals and buildings from memory.

As he approached adolescence, Koestner grew increasingly self-conscious. Once outgoing and eager to give oral book reports and participate in school pageants, he now found speaking in front of the class different. Neither athletic nor competitive, he shunned school recreational activities and games. He preferred to sit by himself and watch the sun's glow on a barn at the far end of the playing field.

"I turned inward, becoming a loner," he says.

Koestner increasingly felt his father's, and to some extent his mother's, disappointment in him. His art interest, combined with a tendency to wander off and seek isolation, became the subject of family talk. Once, while painting in his upstairs bedroom, he overheard his Aunt Ruth tell his mother, "Well, Don has always been a different kind of child." He was branded the black sheep of the Koestner and Umbreit clans.

"In adolescence," Koestner says, "I lost all meaningful communication with my parents." He increasingly felt abandoned by his parent's scorn for his artistic gifts and disappointed in their inability to recognize his need to follow his own course. But the clan's disapproval only stiffened his resolve to stay with his art. If creative expression was an uncommon family trait, being stubborn was not.

Koestner coasted through Roosevelt High School in south Minneapolis, ignored homework, and took shop and other easy courses. But his art teachers recognized his ability. One of them, Miss Figge, while discussing with the class a painting by Edward Hopper, turned to him and asked, "Is that what you think, Don?" The attention, offered in front of the class, both flattered and embarrassed him. Another art teacher, Miss Catrine, told him he was so "picky, picky, picky" he would never become a painter, but she recommended him for Saturday classes at the Minneapolis School of Art. A scholarship was later denied him when Miss Catrine told the judge: "He has promise, but he draws too photographically."

While in the Saturday class at the Minneapolis School of Art, Don became acquainted with the museum that adjoined it, and sometimes he rode his bike there on weekends. Another early art resource was the *Saturday Evening Post*, which often featured the work of regionalist painters such as Thomas Hart Benton, Grant Wood, and John Steuart Curry.

When Koestner graduated from high school in June 1941 he received a partial scholarship for a six-week landscape-painting class at the art school. It was his first exposure to oil painting. He got the scholarship through his own initiative, bringing his reluctant mother along to help him make his case with the art school's president, Edmund Kopietz. Don had never talked with the president but knew him from the Saturday classes that Kopietz visited. The president invited them into his office. Don's mother, intimidated by the officialdom of art school, remained silent as Don showed the president some of his pastel drawings. Kopietz, once a drawing instructor at the Art Institute of Chicago, saw promise.

The six-week class, held from 9 A.M. until noon, required each student to work Monday through Friday to complete a 16-by-20-inch painting each week. When Don's teacher recommended a book on the technical aspects of oil painting, he located a copy. Max Doerner's *The Materials of the Artist and Their Use in Painting: With Notes on the Techniques of the Old Masters*, published in 1934, became one of Don's art bibles.

Jack Koestner might have learned from his life experience that education was the better path, but he did not encourage either of his two children to attend college. Perhaps he feared an education would make them something other than who they were. Jack still bristled at his son's art interest and never looked at his drawings and paintings. Soon after Don completed high school, Jack laid down the law. "This art stuff was okay while you were in school," he said, "but now it's time to get a job."

For a while, the artist worked for Dayton's Department Store as a stock boy, then he became a car checker in Minneapolis for Twin City Rapid Transit Streetcar Company. He stood at various intersections in the city to log the car's arrival time and number of riders. It was a tedious job, and for Koestner, a thorough and precise worker, also intolerable because of the casual method of data collection. Given less than a minute, he could not accurately count the passengers. Adding to his aggravation was an erratic work schedule—night shifts or split shifts of 6 to 10 A.M. and 2 to 6 P.M. One day, after six frustrating months, he told his boss, "I can't do this any more" and quit. The job he left had one residual benefit. When he applied, the company required him to have a physical, and the eye exam revealed that he had astigmatism and needed glasses. Wearing glasses eliminated the headaches he had suffered since childhood.

—⚭—

KOESTNER WORKED FOR SEVERAL OTHER EMPLOYERS while waiting to be drafted for service in World War II. Millions of men had already been called since Japan attacked Pearl Harbor on December 7, 1941. By war's end, more than 15 million men and women served in the U. S. military—10 million of them drafted. When Koestner's notice arrived in May 1943 he was working in the fur storage department of Powers Department Store.

Inducted into the U.S. Army at Fort Snelling on June 7, 1943, Koestner was assigned basic training with an engineering division at Jefferson Barracks near St. Louis. Slightly built, he was apprehensive about the rigors of training but soon found he could hold his own. Being lean was less a disadvantage than carrying excess weight, and he was not short on energy and strength, thanks to his bicycle. When not in physical training, he attended lectures and slide presentations on construction techniques used in building military bases. He found the order and discipline of military life appealing. Even the food was good, he thought, and his weight increased to 140 pounds, the heaviest he would ever be.

Assigned later to the U.S. Army Air Forces, Koestner sought training as a draftsman. He got schooling in Florida, then was sent to North Carolina for two months of training for overseas operations. Not long after that, he was sent to Newport News, Virginia, for transit overseas. Just before his troopship sailed for England—a staging area for the invasion of Europe—he was pulled off because he had not been issued government eyeglasses. Reassigned to another ship, he wound up in Casablanca. He arrived in the Moroccan city on Easter morning 1944. Eighteen months earlier, Allied naval forces had fought a ferocious three-day air and naval campaign there before destroying the Vichy French fleet and coastal garrison. Now the city was peaceful, its white buildings shimmering in the sun. For a week, he explored its raucous bazaars and narrow, winding streets. Then he boarded a troop train that took him several hundred miles northeast through Morocco's Atlas Mountains and northern coastal range to the Mediterranean city of Oran, Algeria. It rained continuously, and the leaky World War I vintage French boxcar he shared with 20 other soldiers had two inches of water on the straw-covered floor. More interested in admiring the mist-shrouded mountains and lush valleys through the open door, he slept little. He enjoyed looking at distant hills and terraced fields—even in the rain. When he did nap, he sat on his helmet.

Oran had been struck by an Allied firestorm on the same day as Casablanca. Now it was secure. Koestner was there two weeks, exploring the city and countryside on foot while waiting for a British troopship that would take him along the Mediterranean, through the Suez Canal into the Red Sea to the Gulf of Aden, and then across the Arabian Sea to Bombay. En route, he vowed that if he survived the war he would become an artist. He spent three weeks in Bombay, bought a sketchpad and pencils, and in his bunk at night—still self-conscious about drawing in public—drew what he remembered seeing during the day. On June 6, 1944, while he floated in a saltwater swimming pool at an English country club, news came of the Normandy invasion. Friends came to call it "the Koestner luck."

Enroute to China, Koestner traveled across India on a British troop train. The train stopped for meals so the soldiers could disembark through side doors to reach the mess car. They ate standing up, then emptied scraps from their mess kits into the outstretched arms of impoverished Indian women who held out, basin-like, the loose folds of their saris. He had never seen such poverty. In India's northeast frontier, he traveled slowly by steamboat up the Brahmaputra River to the Burmese border. Indian boatmen stood on the bow, tossing out lines to measure the shallow river's depth.

At the Burmese border Koestner was airlifted by C-47 transport plane over the 20,000-foot-high Himalayas ("the Hump") to the city of Kunming in southeastern China. There he was assigned to the U. S. Air Forces' 23rd Fighter Control Squadron in Lüliang—part of the 14th Air Force that flew P-40 and P-51 fighter planes and B-29 and B-51 bombers from several small bases in China. The trip from Newport News to Lüliang had taken nearly three months.

Until the end of the war in China, Koestner drew maps. He enlarged existing maps by hand, adding grid lines that would enable ground commanders to pinpoint radar sightings of Japanese aircraft. Koestner doubts that his carefully drawn maps were ever utilized. Radar, a technology introduced early in the war in the Pacific and European theaters of war, never reached China. That was not surprising. The Allied European and Pacific operations had priority on manpower and materiel. The largely undermanned and undersupplied China-Burma-India theater came to be called the "forgotten war." Once the Japanese cut off the Burmese section of the Burma Road in an attempt to isolate China, Allied operations were supplied exclusively from the air. The U.S. Air Transport Command flew fuel, ammunition, food, and other vital supplies over the Himalayas from Allied bases in India.

Japanese planes, based 200 miles north of Lüliang, routinely bombed the runways of American air bases. The morning following a raid, Chinese work gangs rebuilt the damaged runways by hand. Buffalo carts carried boulders to the site, and hundreds of coolies—men, women, and children—picked at the boulders with hammers and sticks to make gravel to fill the bomb holes. Then, working in large teams, they pulled enormous rollers over the pulverized stones to smooth the surface. Entire runways were originally built that way. At Luliang, the crushed rock runway was a mile long, perhaps fifty feet wide, and six feet deep.

Koestner was reassigned to several U.S. Army air bases in China, continuing to make his "useless" radar maps. To reach one of the bases required a three-day, 400-mile jeep trip on the China leg of the mountainous Burma Road from its terminus at Kunming. Traveling to another base, his railroad car was one of several at the back of the train that jumped the tracks and had to be abandoned. Unable to squeeze himself into any of the other jam-packed cars, he rode the engine's cowcatcher the remaining 15 miles to his destination. The Japanese lines were only a hundred miles farther east.

Koestner wrote to his parents from his base halfway around the world, describing his experience. At the top of his letters he made drawings of rickshas, coolies, water buffalos, and other exotic features of the Chinese landscape—a journal of sorts that the artist treasured but his orderly mother did not; she discarded his letters.

Near the end of the war with Japan, Koestner made radar maps for a possible invasion of Taiwan. After his tour in China, which ended with the Japanese surrender in August 1945, he was reassigned to the states. His return journey from China—this time he sailed from Calcutta instead of Bombay—was the reverse of his journey there. After a full month in transit he had a month's furlough, which he spent in Minneapolis. His orders were to report afterward to San Diego for possible duty in the Pacific. On the way west from Minneapolis his discharge number came up and in San Diego, on January 3, 1946, he was discharged as a sergeant. He received $80 travel pay to return home, bought a $30 coach fare, and saved the rest.

During his 31-month tour of military duty, Koestner, though

sometimes near the enemy while in China, never saw him up close, never fired a shot, never felt he accomplished anything useful. But the experience opened his eyes to the world, assured him a college education, and set him on the course of his choosing.

If a man does not keep pace with his companions,
perhaps it is because he hears a different drummer.
Let him step to the music which he hears,
however measured or far away.

Henry David Thoreau

Fundamentals

MEN AND WOMEN RETURNING from military service at the end of World War II faced a difficult adjustment. Some found their overseas experience had profoundly changed them. Those who went into uniform not long after high school came back with different values and priorities. That so many returned to civilian life at the same time created a sense of urgency to "get ahead" and "build a better life."

Don Koestner felt out of step. Although he had grown up during the 1930s depression he did not feel the postwar pull of settling down and making money that many of his generation did, and he resisted any pressure to do so. His relationship with his parents, particularly his father, was strained and detached. The two men seldom talked, but Jack expected his son to find a permanent job that paid a respectable wage. Jack envied his son's future in the expanding postwar economy as well as the job opportunities and purchasing power that lay before him. From what he observed, veterans joining the robust workforce could secure a GI loan for a tract home in one of the fast-growing suburbs west of the city, maybe buy a new Willys-Overland Jeep station wagon, get a 12-foot fishing boat with a 5-horsepower motor, marry, start a family, and receive company-paid vacations. When Don told his dad he was going to pursue art studies, the gap between them widened. "Nevertheless," Don said, "my parents loved me enough to offer me a place to stay while going to art school."

Don Koestner reconnected with his cousins Art Koestner and Roy and Arnie Ehlert with whom he had bicycled Dakota County roads and gone to movies as a teenager. All were veterans, but in reuniting they talked little of their service experiences. Roy began dating a girl shortly after his return, and because he and Don had been close before the war, Roy sometimes included him on dates for the movies. When Don started art school in the fall of 1946, he began dating a girl in his class, and the two couples double-dated for a while.

Artists—at least those in the traditional art world Koestner respected—were craftspersons at their core. Not those of Jack Koestner's world, but people who nevertheless applied themselves to their tasks and put in a good day's work. Serious painters, Don Koestner was certain, did not wait for inspiration to move them to action. This was the practical voice of his ancestors; he was wading in a Teutonic gene pool. Someone had told him, and he believed it, that a German is born with a hammer in hand. He wished his father could see the connection between his skills as a mechanic and handyman and his son's as an artist and recognize their common love of precision and attention to detail, their common seriousness. But Jack Koestner saw no similarity. In his view, working men grew calluses on their hands and artists flitted and twittered. Father and son faced each other across a widening cultural divide.

Soon after returning to civilian life in early 1946, Don Koestner took a warehouse job with John Deere and Company, filling orders for tractor parts. He planned to enroll at the Minneapolis School of Art (MSA) that fall but didn't tell his employer. When he quit in September, his boss was upset. Koestner said, "He assumed he had another forty-year man on his payroll."

That summer, Koestner also worked part time as a mechanic in a small garage near Roy Ehlert's parents' home in Minneapolis. While employed there he was able to rebuild the engine of a 1932 Plymouth he had bought before he was drafted in 1943. Now he installed oversized pistons to cure the vintage auto's "piston slap" and made other needed repairs. He had acquired such mechanical skills over the years by helping his father work on a succession of secondhand family cars. When Koestner left the garage to start college, the garage owner confided to Ehlert, "I think Don is making a mistake going to art school; he would make a good mechanic."

Koestner attended MSA on the GI Bill, one of nearly 8 million World War II veterans who took advantage of the government vocational training and higher education program. He received $60 a month, plus college tuition fees. To make ends meet, he worked Saturday afternoons in the Minneapolis Institute of Arts coatroom—the college and museum were joined by a tunnel— hanging up coats and keeping track of museum attendance for 60 cents an hour.

Throughout his college years, Koestner lived at home in an

upstairs apartment his parents had sublet during the war years. The comfortable quarters included a bedroom, bath, and another small bedroom he used as a studio. The arrangement, though he paid his parents a modest amount for room and board, was a generous accommodation—especially since his parents believed he was hopelessly adrift.

—m—

THE MINNEAPOLIS SCHOOL OF ART was founded in 1886 as the Minneapolis School of Fine Arts (MSFA). It was the offspring of the Minneapolis Society of Fine Arts, incorporated three years earlier to promote "a knowledge and love of art in the community." The school was modeled after the best art schools in America, those often associated with leading art museums: the Boston Museum of Fine Arts, the Metropolitan Museum of Art, the Art Institute of Chicago. Their method of teaching was an American adaptation of a highly structured regimen developed during the early nineteenth century by European art academies. The school's first director was trained in Europe in the academic tradition.

Douglas Volk, hired in 1886, implanted "the academic method in Minneapolis." The school's first home was a rented house on Hennepin Avenue, near Tenth Street. Attending its first four-month session were 28 students—26 of them women. The latter sat at their easels in long dresses with long sleeves, their hair piled atop their heads and held in place with whalebone combs. In 1889, the art school moved to the top floor of the new Minneapolis Public Library on the corner of Hennepin Avenue and Tenth Street.

The son of an American sculptor working abroad, Volk spent his boyhood studying art in Rome and Venice, then at 18 continued his education in Paris at the École des Beaux-Arts under Jean-Léon Gérôme. He capped his four-year training with Gérôme with the exhibit of a painting at the Salon de Paris of 1878. He then returned to the United States to teach at Cooper Union in New York City, where he taught for seven years until recruited for the Minneapolis position.

With the support of the school's directors, Volk made clear the school's objectives. These were to teach the elements, principles, and practice of art as taught "in the best art schools." He was specific about what the art school would not teach, including "any of the minor specialties and adaptations of art." He also vowed that "no instructors will be employed but those of the best education, experience, and repute."

The "academic method" Volk promoted emphasized proficiency in drawing the human figure. Art students spent their first months drawing the human figure from etchings and engravings (elementary class), then from plaster casts of classical statues (antique class), and then, after a year or so, from a live model (life class). Volk's drawing classes using nude models met with resistance from first-year students, the majority of them young women who insisted that the model be fully draped. Volk reluctantly consented. Advancement from one level of his challenging classes to the next was not guaranteed. Some students repeated the beginning classes several times.

The 1886 catalog of the Minneapolis School of Fine Arts (the art school's first) describes the rigorous training regimen that Volk introduced as director and principal teacher:

> Instruction will be offered in drawing from the object and antique; in painting from the cast and from still life; and in drawing and painting from the draped model or living head. . . . Instruction in composition will also be given to pupils sufficiently advanced. Sufficient training in the above course will enable the student to apply his knowledge and skill to all branches and specialties of art in a thorough and intelligent

manner. As a foundation for landscape painting, such a course is indispensable.

To the above, Volk added: "Landscape painting as a specialty is not taught in the leading art schools, and is not taught in this school. The only place possible to study it is from nature, after one has learned the rudiments common to all branches of art."

But the art school's emphasis soon had to adapt to changing times and fiscal priorities—at least to those in Minnesota. By the end of its first decade of operation, the school's tuition-derived income was not covering expenses, including Volk's salary. A better teacher than administrator, Volk left after seven years, but not before hiring his replacement.

Robert Koehler was a German-born artist raised in Milwaukee but trained in Munich. For a time he had made his living as a commercial printmaker. In 1899, as director of the MSFA, he added a department of decorative design to meet a broader range of student interests. Courses offered ranged from embroidery to woodworking—not machine-oriented crafts suited for manufacturing but skilled handicrafts that were rooted in the popular Victorian Arts and Crafts movement. To reflect its broader mission, in 1910 the school changed its name from the Minneapolis School of Fine Arts to the Minneapolis School of Art (MSA).

In 1915, the school became part of the new Minneapolis Institute of Arts complex at 24th Street, between Stevens and Third Avenue. Clinton Morrison donated this 10-acre tract, valued at $250,000, in January 1911. It was the original Morrison family homestead, known as Villa Rosa. Following the announcement of Morrison's gift of land, William Hood Dunwoody, president of the Washburn Crosby Company (later General Mills) and president of the Fine Arts Society, promised $100,000 toward construction of a museum and school, his gift conditional on other benefactors stepping forward. At a dinner of society members on January 10, 1911, an additional $250,000 was pledged, and by the end of that month the remaining money was raised to meet the $537,000 construction estimate. (Society members included eight of the city's sixteen millionaires: Morrison, Dunwoody, Russell M. Bennett, John B. Gilfillan, Thomas Lowry, Clinton Frank H. Peavey, John S. Pillsbury, and Thomas B. Walker.) When William Dunwoody died in 1914, his will provided a million dollar gift to be used only for the purchase of works of art.

The art school now developed its curriculum around two training programs: fine arts and applied arts. Although both departments stressed a foundation in good drawing and other fundamentals, the emphasis shifted from the traditional model to one more focused on meeting the vocational needs of a broader range of students.

Some older members of the governing society's board expressed concern about students' seeming lack of interest in the museum's collections—paintings, drawings, tapestries, and other artworks they had sponsored with personal gifts. A note in the 1915-16 school catalog addressed the issue: "All students are expected to visit at frequent intervals the Minneapolis Institute of Arts in order to familiarize themselves with . . . its permanent collection."

Over several generations, the abandonment of "academic training" in art fundamentals had produced a knowledge gap. Art teachers—in high schools and colleges as well as in art schools—could not teach drawing and painting skills that they had not mastered themselves. By the 1940s, the scope of instruction at the Minneapolis School of Art had broadened to include courses in costume design, fashion illustration, interior design, advertising art, design for industry, photography, and mechanical drafting.

Entering the Minneapolis School of Art in 1946, Koestner had a rude awakening. "Initially I was a timid and naïve student, in awe of the 'real artists' who were my instructors," he said. "But disillusionment set in during my second year. I began to realize that instruction was haphazard and in some areas nonexistent. I also began to realize I could not admire the work being done by my instructors." He was a twentieth-century man seeking the nineteenth-century art training that in 50 years had virtually disappeared.

Koestner got to know several students who shared his disappointment. One of them, Richard Lack, was four years younger than he but "could draw better and knew more about the history of art than our instructors." The group also included fellow veterans Charles (Chuck) Gravem, Vince Peterson, and Cliff Moen. The group met regularly at the Nicollet Cafe, a nearby art school hangout where they "drank beer and talked about the usual things guys in art school talk about—girls and art." But also about literature, music, and theater. In this small circle of students, Koestner found a camaraderie and intellectual companionship he had never known. Until then, he said, "I knew nothing of the rich history of art—not even the names of the Old Masters, other than Rembrandt." The students became lifelong friends.

Koestner and his fellow discontents—most a few years older than other students because of their military service—enjoyed cordial relations with their instructors despite their low regard for their work as artists. From their perspective as students seeking traditional art training, their instructors' work reflected poor drawing skills. And their lectures on painting revealed how little they knew about color and paint-handling.

Koestner absorbed what he could at MSA, supplementing his education with visits to museum collections at every opportunity. During school breaks he took road trips across the country, sometimes with art-school friends. The museum visits allowed him to view original paintings up close and to do his own studies. There, he could see the actual buildup of paint on the canvases and examine brushstrokes. He began a lifelong process of teaching himself through observation and practice.

In the summer of 1948, Don Koestner and Cliff Moen toured the southern and eastern United States for three months in Moen's 1931 Model A Ford. At the time, Koestner owned a 1933 Hupmobile, a low-slung sedan resembling a movie gangster's getaway car, but it was expensive to run and more trouble-prone than Moen's older but more reliable and simple-to-repair Ford.

Koestner and Moen were alumni of Roosevelt High School in Minneapolis, though Moen had been three grades behind Koestner. Both liked to travel. On this trip, the two adventurers drove single-lane roads—major construction of the federal Interstate system didn't begin until 1956— that took them into the heart of the country. Along the way they slept in war-surplus, one-man pup tents, used outdoor privies at campsites and country schoolhouses, and bathed in rivers. The latter sometimes required persistence. In Arkansas one afternoon, a park caretaker kept them from using the river to wash up. They left and slept that night behind a billboard. The next morning, early, they returned to the river. They could see the caretaker watching them from his house, but this time he didn't bother to chase them away.

Moen's oil-guzzling Model A required a quart refill every two hours (as opposed to every so many miles), so they bought cheap, "re-refined" oil in bulk for 10 cents a quart. Gas was 25 cents a gallon, sometimes less. One service station in Philadelphia sold them a gallon of war-surplus oil for 50 cents—*World War I* oil! Their car ran dependably until they reached St. Louis, when the generator burned out. From then on, they stuck to a daylight schedule. At night, they parked the car at the top of an incline so they could push-start it the next morning.

The two travelers usually ate in small town cafes and restaurants. Moen recalls that 60 cents bought a breakfast of bacon, eggs, and hash browns and for supper a hot beef or pork sandwich. Koestner remembers a stretch of the Blue Ridge Parkway in Virginia that was still under construction in 1948 and without the amenities that would later develop. Unable to find restaurants, they bought a few cans of baked beans in a country store and improvised a meal. Lacking a camp stove, they gathered wood scraps along the construction site and built a small fire. Minus a can opener, they punched holes around the top of the cans with nails they had also scavenged; their hammer was the Model A's tire iron. They ate their beans, heated in the cans, with wooden spoons Koestner carved with his jackknife. Along the way they stopped to do casein sketches on 15-by-20-inch illustration boards. They were able to sell some of the paintings for five dollars each, allowing them to buy an occasional fresh-baked pie and quart of ice cream. Moen, who relished the adventure of the open road, remembered Koestner's "seriousness about art" and his passion for studying paintings. They visited major museums in St. Louis, New Orleans, Washington, Baltimore, Philadelphia, New York, and Toronto.

The next summer, 1949, Koestner visited the Chicago Art Institute and also museums in Detroit, Toledo, and Des Moines. He covered his expenses for this trip with a $100 Van Derlip travel and study scholarship he received at MSA. (The scholarship was named for Ethel Morrison Van Derlip, a second-generation benefactor.) That fall, he and several others returned to Chicago for a Van Gogh show.

Koestner read whatever he could find about the artists whose work he admired. At this time in his development, they included the highly developed portraits of Hans Holbein. Koestner did drawings of them at the Toledo Museum of Art. He also enjoyed

Pieter Bruegel's storytelling paintings, such as *The Blind Leading the Blind*. A poster-size reproduction of the sixteenth-century masterpiece hung on the tunnel wall connecting MSA and the Minneapolis Institute of Arts. The irony of the title "was not lost on me," Koestner says.

Koestner was attracted to the technical side of painting, perhaps another echo of his German genes. One day, in the art institute's bookstore, he and Richard Lack discovered a book with an intriguing title: *The Secret Formulas and Techniques of the Masters*. Published in 1948, it was written by Jacques Maroger, an art restorer and former technical director of the Louvre Museum. Through painstaking scientific analysis, the restorer worked to recapture the practices of master painters working before 1700. In their works he saw qualities of color and modeling and a brilliance of surface not present in master paintings of the eighteenth and nineteenth centuries. Maroger's book, more intriguing to Koestner than a mystery novel, included a formula for preparing an oil medium from dry, hand-ground pigments. Paints made in this time-tested way were not only more durable but dried faster and produced colors of greater intensity. Both Koestner and Lack bought a copy. *Secret Formulas* joined Max Doerner's book, *Materials of the Artist and Their Use in Painting*, on Koestner's bookshelf of treasured painting manuals.

Disappointed in the art school's training, Koestner focused on becoming more knowledgeable about his craft through personal studies of museum collections. Pressing on him as he approached graduation was the problem of making a living with an art style considered to be out of vogue. The modernist movement was largely born in the 1920s with Pablo Picasso's abstract painting style and through the establishment of the Museum of Modern Art in Manhattan. These powerful cultural forces became the standard-bearers of visual art. Modernism made earlier art styles seem old-fashioned and lacking in message. Art critics and educators, as well as most young artists, regarded traditional painting as something without relevance to the current day. The modern credo became: "Art must move on."

Upon graduation from art school in June 1950, Koestner received a second Van Derlip scholarship. The $400 award, modest by today's standards, was equal to four month's wages for working full time at 75 cents an hour. The windfall enabled him to take a two-month road trip to visit museums in Chicago, Toledo, Boston, New York, and Washington, D.C. The scholarship arrived in two payments, with $200 awarded at the start of his journey in mid-August. Edmund Kopietz had instructed Koestner to write when he arrived in New York of what he had learned from his museum visits, and to provide a hotel address at which he could receive the remaining $200 check.

Koestner was nearly broke when he reached New York City. Even his car, a 1936 Chevrolet he had bought from his cousin Arnie Ehlert for $200, seemed on its last legs. After paying for his room in advance, the artist had almost nothing to live on from Friday until Monday when the second check was to arrive. On Saturday he "foolishly bought a candy bar." That left him 12 cents. On Sunday morning he went to a delicatessen down the street and blew it all on a small loaf of bread. He still had a little gas, so he drove to the Hudson River and parked while he munched on a piece of bread. A panhandler knocked on his window. "I don't have any money—but you can have a piece of bread if you want," the good Samaritan said. The beggar rejected the offer of food and walked away.

On Monday the check arrived, along with a student news pamphlet proclaiming "Don Koestner is in New York." "I felt I was on top of the world," Koestner later recalled. He got into his car to find a bank to cash the check, but as he nosed onto the street, the car ran out of gas. He pushed it back into its parking spot and returned to his hotel. After pleading his trustworthiness to the hotel manager, the man cashed it. Koestner splurged that day, buying art supplies and books, and a hot meal in a neighborhood cafe. Then he found a garage that for three dollars installed new points in his exhausted Chevrolet.

After four years of art school, Koestner felt he was just beginning his quest to become a landscape painter. His goal was to continue the journey—to live and to paint. He already had a plan in motion and was eager to return home.

Art is not a thing; it is a way.
Elbert Hubbard

Independence Day

DON KOESTNER WAS AT A CROSSROADS. Twenty-six years old when he completed art school in June 1950, he knew that he had much to learn about painting. His dilemma was how to master his craft and also eat.

In art school, he became aware of commercial art that offered lucrative careers in advertising and publishing. This was art as business. Not that fine artists were exempt from the practical necessities of selling their work. He hoped his art would find an appreciative audience, but becoming rich and famous had little bearing on his interest in painting. He painted to paint, yet earning a living could not be ignored.

A week or so before graduation, a college friend lent Koestner her copy of Henry David Thoreau's *Walden,* an inspiring book about living a simple existence close to nature. The book's impact was immediate and lasting. More than an inspiration, Thoreau provided him with a path.

Thoreau built a cabin on Walden Pond, near Concord, Massachusetts, in 1845. He lived there for two years and two months and wrote about his experience in a book that took him eight years to complete.

"Simplify, simplify," he counseled in his famous work. Spend your time doing what gives meaning to your life rather than wasting your energy just to sustain a life of excess. Live deliberately.

Koestner found much to relate to in Thoreau's book. He enjoyed the challenge of getting by with the bare necessities. He was comfortable with solitude. And although he did not want a hermit's life, being alone fit his temperament. Like his father and uncles and cousins, he was resourceful—able to build things he needed and do routine maintenance.

In reading Thoreau, Koestner found his choice becoming clear: If he lived in a city like New York, Chicago, or Minneapolis, he would need to work a five-day week just to pay his rent and cover the expenses of urban living. This would leave him little time to paint. But if he adopted a simple lifestyle he would have more time and energy for his art. He would need some income, but perhaps he could meet basic needs by working two days a week rather than five. The key was to avoid debt and hold down expenses.

At the art school's graduation party in June, he told the friend who had lent him *Walden:* "A year from now I'll be living in a cabin in the woods."

To achieve his goal of independence, Koestner needed land. Enabling his search was a windfall—a $500 commission from St.

Olaf Catholic Church in downtown Minneapolis to paint a three-paneled mural; the subject was the life of Birgitta of Sweden, saint of the northern kingdoms. The recently retired Edmund Kopietz, president of the art school since 1928, had recommended him for the project. Kopietz had helped arrange earlier awards and scholarships for the industrious and serious-minded Koestner as far back as high school. Koestner completed the mural that summer; when the church burned two years later, the mural was destroyed.

Jack Koestner, despite his low regard for "art foolishness," admired his son's interest in finding a place in the country. He, too, had wanted to live on the land—an unrealized dream. As an outdoorsman and amateur horticulturist, he thought his son's interest in land was practical and down to earth.

Jack suggested Don look for property on the Mississippi River near Hastings, where the two of them had once fished for perch and bullheads. Their fishing spot was a widening of the river called Spring Lake, a spring-fed marsh until a dam built in the 1930s by the U. S. Army Corps of Engineers joined the two. Talking about it, father and son both remembered seeing paddle-wheel steamboats pass beyond a ridge of trees separating the river and lake. Jack also recalled a gristmill and house, built in the 1880s. He knew the mill was gone, swept away by a flood some years before, but he thought the house might still be there.

"Maybe you could buy it," he said.

Looking for the mill house on July 4, 1950, Koestner drove his 14-year-old Chevrolet along a township gravel road to a boat landing on the Mississippi River. He ended up at Walt's Cave, a tavern fronting a hundred-foot-long cavern. Locals said the cave, originally used to cool beer in the summertime, was carved into the sandstone bluff by a work gang of Civil War prisoners using pick axes.

Koestner asked the bartender whether he knew of any property for sale and was told about the "Jeremy place" on the bluff. He drove to the top and stumbled into a Jeremy picnic—for generations a Fourth of July family gathering. The family had settled on the bluff in the 1870s, sometime after Alexander Jeremy came up the river in a skiff to operate a stone quarry and later a sawmill on the riverbank.

Two of the pioneer's sons still lived on the property. William Horton Jeremy, known locally as both Hort Jeremy and Captain Jeremy, was a picturesque character in his seventies, fond of wearing a white suit on special occasions to maintain his former image as pilot of a paddle wheeler. When Koestner met him, the captain was seated in a decrepit rocking chair, his white suit stained and rumpled. Koestner stated his interest in buying some land. Without hesitation, the captain said he had a 250-foot lot he'd sell for $225. To encourage his prospect, he quickly offered a bonus. "It's got a well on it."

A short time later, Koestner met Hort Jeremy's younger brother, Rex. Although the brothers lived together, they did not get along, and Rex took Koestner aside.

"Offer him $500, and he'll give you the rest of the block-and-a-half he owns," Rex whispered.

Koestner bought the entire parcel of roughly five acres. He was elated about owning so much land and the prospect of building on it. He felt a special connection with that landscape. As a teenager, he had bicycled from Minneapolis with his cousins along Dakota County roads just south of the bluff. So the area, he said later, was "indelibly stamped in my memory." Finding a secluded spot so quickly exemplified Don's "Koestner luck." Soon he'd have his own Walden, where he could live deliberately and simply. It was a Walden without a pond, but the Mississippi River was an acceptable substitute.

—ᴍ—

A BEND IN THE RIVER ZIGZAGGING SOUTH beyond St. Paul, past Newport, St. Paul Park, and Grey Cloud Island defined the north-facing bluff. The larger tract of land making up Koestner's five-acre Walden was once part of another man's dream. A century earlier, Ignatius Donnelly had envisioned a town there. Donnelly came to Minnesota Territory from Philadelphia in 1853 at the age of 22 with dreams of building a utopian community. The lawyer soon formed a partnership with real estate developer John Nininger, a fellow Pennsylvanian who also came west looking for opportunity.

Donnelly and Nininger bought 474 acres, then surveyed and platted the tract as Nininger City (locally pronounced Ninnin-jer). They divided it into 3,800 lots and priced them at $6 apiece. The two speculators hoped Nininger would become a major river port settled by immigrants from the East, whom Donnelly would enlist with his Emigrant Aid Association. The payment of 25 one-dollar installments entitled an association member to a free ticket to Nininger City, a brief period of support, and a few tools to help the member become self-sustaining. To promote the development, Donnelly published a newspaper, *The Emigrant Aid Journal.*

Donnelly, from heavily German-settled Pennsylvania, was particularly interested in attracting German immigrants. He knew them to be industrious, resourceful, and hardworking—important qualities for building a community. But his dream for a great city faded when in the late summer of 1857 the nation headed into a financial panic, much of it triggered by land and railroad speculation. Fears of an economic depression, fueled by eastern newspapers, undermined public confidence in new ventures. Nationally, the land grant program stalled. In Minnesota, local banks failed. One casualty was the proposed Nininger, St. Peter and Western Railroad that was to bridge the Mississippi River at Nininger City to enable the flow of immigrants and stimulate the new town's growth. Within months, the once promising town began to decline. The final death knell tolled when the railroad chose to bridge the river at Hastings, three miles downriver. Nininger City's homes and buildings were moved or abandoned, its streets and yards slowly reverting to pasture and fields.

Though disappointed that his vision never materialized, Donnelly remained in Nininger City (later renamed Nininger township), practiced law in Hastings, and represented Minnesota in Congress during the Civil War. The "Sage of Nininger" died on January 1, 1901. His personal property once adjoined the parcel that Koestner bought from Captain Jeremy in 1950; the long-abandoned Donnelly mansion was razed just two years before.

In October 1950, back from his two-month road trip east, Koestner scouted the want ads for salvaged lumber with which he could build his cabin the next summer. He responded to an ad: "$40 takes all—used lumber." The wood came from an old fraternity house torn down on the University of Minnesota campus. The seller built his own house with most of it, and Koestner bought what was left. There appeared to be enough material to frame the 14-by-22-foot cabin he'd drawn up. He also got windows and a door. With the help of his three cousins, he hauled the salvaged lumber to Nininger. He'd remove the nails in the spring.

Again, Thoreau provided Koestner his inspiration. Although the New England writer had felled several white pines for his cabin frame, he had found his siding on a shanty he bought in Concord. "An uncommonly fine one," Thoreau said of the shack. He took it down board by board and removed the nails. He then spread the boards on the grass by the pond "to bleach and warp back again in the sun." Koestner liked the concept of reusing lumber; the practice minimized cutting healthy trees and cut waste.

That winter (1950–51)—a big snow year—Koestner drove for the Richfield Cab Company, a suburban Minneapolis taxi service, to earn money for lumber and general building expenses and to fund future art trips. He began the job on December 1, 1950, continuing to live with his parents. By then, Jack and Frieda had moved to the less-settled Minneapolis suburb of Bloomington, south of Richfield, where Jack could have a garden. One winter afternoon, Don Koestner visited Nininger with his cousin Roy Ehlert, and the two of them skied from the road onto his property over the tops of fences. Ehlert, though he had risked his life as a B-24 tail gunner on bombing raids over Germany during World War II, was sensible and practical and thought Koestner's prospects uncertain at best.

"How are you going to live out here, once you get the cabin built?" he asked.

"I don't know," Koestner said, "I'm just going to see what happens."

Koestner rarely concerned himself with a host of what-ifs before deciding to act. It was enough for him to set a plan in motion. He was not reckless but generally optimistic. There was an excitement about not knowing every turn in the road. In explaining his attitude, he paraphrased American painter Albert Ryder, who likened himself to an inchworm on the end of a branch, reaching into space for a footing he could not quite touch. Both living and painting were like that for Koestner. His boyhood excursions and later military travels overseas had contributed to his comfort level with the unknown. Don Koestner saw himself as more adventurous and relaxed, more of a risk taker than his cautious father, Jack.

"My dad," he said, "would not set out for a weekend drive to Uncle Frank's farm in Becker without first listening to Cedric Adams's weather report on WCCO radio."

Photo Section I

Family of Ernst and Wilhelmina Umbreit, circa 1908. Frieda Umbreit
(Don Koestner's mother) on far right.

Frieda Umbreit
Koestner

John William
Koestner

Wedding portrait of Don's parents,
John and Frieda Koestner, April 6, 1918.

Don Koestner, confirmation,
circa 1936.

Fifth and sixth grade class of Sibley Grade School, St. Paul, 1934. Don Koestner, second
row, far left.

Left: Don Koestner, age 11, at Camp Shady Trails, Traverse City, Michigan.

Center: Don Koestner, right, biking with cousin Arnie Ehlert, near Lake Josephine, circa 1936.

Bottom: Don Koestner on his Montgomery Ward bicycle, 1936.

Left: Pvt. Don Koestner at Drew Field, near Tampa, Florida, for overseas training, 1943.

Below: Exploring Luliang, in southeastern China, 1944.

Above: Children of Luliang.

Right: Don Koestner taking a break on base.

Chinese laborers laying rock bed for airfield runway.

P-51 Mustang fighter planes lined up along runway, part of U.S. Air Forces 23rd Fighter Control Squadron at Luliang.

Flight control tower showing elevation of Luliang airfield.

Top left: Jack and Frieda Koestner's Minneapolis home, 3932 40th Ave. S., 1940s. Don occupied an upstairs apartment while attending art school.

Top right: Jack Koestner, an amateur horticulturist, in his garden.

Don and cousins Arnie and Roy Ehlert walk across log-jammed Pigeon River at the Canadian border, Memorial Day 1946.

The Koestner and Ehlert cousins, all veterans of WWII, gather on Christmas 1946. From left, Don Koestner, Arnie Ehlert, Roy Ehlert, and Art Koestner.

Students on steps of Morrison Building, Minneapolis School of Art, 1946.

Right: Don Koestner, left, and fellow students in life-drawing classroom.

Below: Don Koestner on fender of 1931 Plymouth purchased while in high school and stored in a neighbor's garage during his military service.

Below: Don and date ice skate on Minnehaha Creek, Minneapolis.

Don Koestner car camping in northern Minnesota, summer 1946, before starting art school.

Koestner's self-maintained 1931 Plymouth.

During Easter vacation, 1948, Don Koestner and Cliff Moen do a test-run with Cliff's 1931 Model A Ford for a planned summer-long road trip through the southern and eastern United States.

Above: Cliff between their pup tents in country school yard, northern Iowa.

Below: The artists test their ability to sell paintings on the road (with no takers).

Above: Don Koestner sketches in pen and ink, Beardstown, Illinois, during 1948 summer road trip.

Right: Cliff Moen beside marker commemorating 1858 "A House Divided" speech by Abraham Lincoln, Springfield, Illinois.

Below: Koestner adds engine oil to Moen's Model A Ford.

Above: Don Koestner bathes in Ozark Mountains river.

Left: Koestner at crossroads in Mississippi.

Below: Cliff Moen and Don Koestner reach Miami city limits.

Right: Ford Model A maintenance and reorganization in Florida.

Center: Drying clothes on roof of wayside shelter.

Bottom: Don makes oil sketch of Pennsylvania town.

Don Koestner studies master paintings in museum, a key component of his art education.

Don Koestner canoeing on the St. Croix River with art school friend
Joyce Houser, 1949.

Don Koestner, left, and helper clear site for building cabin in Nininger, 1951.

Floor joists made of salvaged lumber.

Koestner's art school friends
Vince Peterson, left, and
Chuck Gravem, right, get
counsel in river salvaging from
Rex Jeremy. Rex leans on his
"pick pole," used to snag
lumber in the river.

Koestner's "Walden," summer 1951, completely framed and solidly sided with boards
from a $40-takes-all sale. The cabin floor measured 14 by 22 feet. The car is Koestner's
1939 Chrysler.

Koestner's outhouse was salvaged from an old farm in Richfield, Minnesota. He hauled it to Nininger by trailer, with the help of his cab company employer, Pete Peterson.

Koestner sits beside cabin door, autumn 1951. The Mississippi River flows behind him.

The river-facing north side of the completed cabin with a covering of waterproof sheeting imprinted with a brick pattern.

Koestner *(far right)* saws firewood near cabin's east entrance.

Above: A large elm tree partially frames Koestner's Nininger cabin. Rex Jeremy claimed that his father's leg, amputated years earlier, was buried at its base.

Right: A night scene of the elm tree painted by Koestner from his cabin window (see photo above) in the winter of 1952-53.

Above: A view of cabin interior, winter 1951-1952. Portrait of Chuck Gravem in progress.

Left: The artist sits at compact gateleg table

Below: Koestner's Chrysler crosses a ravine on a home-made bridge near the cabin.

Kitchen with wood-burning range Koestner bought at an auction.

Koestner works on a portrait beside his north-facing window.

Koestner's heat source was a coal-burning space heater he bought used for $7 and converted to a woodburner. The stovepipe extended below the ceiling and out the wall into a brick-enclosed chimney.

Ink and wash sketch of Don and cabin interior by Cliff Moen.

Don Koestner at his studio easel, Nininger. The three-paned plate-glass window replaced the original multi-paned window.

Koestner empties water from a five-foot length of sheet-metal downspout improvised in 1953 to draw water from an old well. One extraction of the downspout from the 100-foot-deep well filled one bucket with fresh water.

Don Koestner bathing outdoors in a salvaged bathtub. He filled the tub with six inches of well water to warm it in the sun. Just before bathing he added a teakettle of boiling water. The hand pump replaced the tripod and downspout system in 1955.

South view of the cabin, 1955, showing a "stone room" addition and brick fireplace chimney. Bricks and stones were salvaged from several Twin Cities construction projects and hauled to the site in a 1939 bread delivery truck that Koestner bought in a trade for his 1939 Chrysler, plus $40.

Koestner raking fresh gravel on road leading to his cabin. In spring, parts of the road could be ankle-deep in mud.

Rex Jeremy, Don Koestner's bachelor neighbor in Nininger. Rex built Koestner's chimney in exchange for a load of bricks for a fireplace of his own, plus Don's pancake breakfasts during the course of the project.

Painting friends and colleagues Don Koestner and Richard Lack
discuss art at the Mississippi River's edge.

Don Koestner silhouetted against the evening sky.

Europe Bike Trip, 1954

Cliff Moen and Don Koestner on bicycles bought at port of Le Havre. They biked across parts of France, Italy, Austria, and Germany.

Stopping to eat along road to Paris.

The campers find their bikes partially submerged from an all-night rain.

Cliff and Don with another passenger on a river boat in Germany.

Europe Sketches

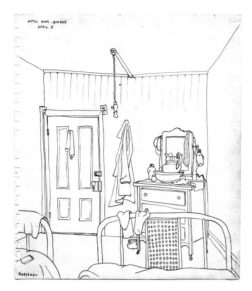

Elderly man.

Pen and ink sketch of Quebec hotel room, April
16, 1954. Don Koestner and Cliff Moen stayed
there before boarding a ship for Europe.

Pen and ink drawing of country home near Paris, April 30, 1954.

Cityscape of Parthenay, France,
May 10, 1954.

Woman resting on bench.

Pen and wash drawing of mountain village in Italy.

Wedding portrait of Fern Bolin and Don Koestner,
June 30, 1960.

Fern and Don at show of Don's
paintings, June 8, 1962. Portrait
of Fern behind them.

Don and Fern cut wedding cake at a post-honey-
moon reception given by friends Jackie and Walter
Gardner at their nearby summer cabin.

Fern with son, Frederick, born January 20, 1963.

Don and Fern celebrate Christmas 1964 with children Fred and Lorna. Lorna was born May 1, 1964.

Above: Don and children with grandparents Frieda and Jack Koestner.

Right: Lorna and Fred in Nininger, 1966.

Left: Fred and Lorna, 1968. Fireplace in "stone room" addition.

Below: South side of remodeled cabin after several rooms had been added.

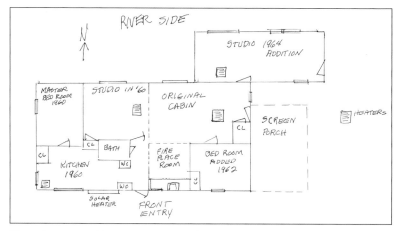

Floor plan recreated by Fern Koestner to show various expansions on the original 14 x 22 foot cabin. Don's 1960 studio became a bedroom after Lorna's birth in 1964. He then built a new studio on the northeast corner of the original cabin.

Koestner's property was half a mile from the road, and he knew he'd be snowed in during winter months. He thought about being alone for long periods of time, but, reassured by his reading of Thoreau, he did not find the prospect daunting.

"I can think of no companion as companionable as solitude," Thoreau had written.

His work cut out for him, Koestner planned to quit his cab-driving job in the spring to concentrate on building his cabin, but the cab owner offered him a weekend schedule, and he accepted. He continued the arrangement for eight years, until 1958. During that period his earnings averaged $15 a weekend; with that he could buy a week's groceries. A small garden of corn, carrots, potatoes, onions, and squash later enabled him to lower his summer food spending to $3 a week.

In April 1951, Koestner pulled nails from his used lumber stockpile and collected other materials as well. Some he bought from Rose Brothers, a salvage yard on Wabasha Street in St. Paul. He also looked to the river—a source he would not have considered but for Rex Jeremy.

Rex was as picturesque as his older brother, Hort Jeremy, and a storyteller; they shared a nearby house shaded by a large American elm. One day Rex told Koestner, "See that tree? That tree got so big because that's where my dad's leg is buried, under that tree."

Their father, Alexander Joseph Jeremy, had had both legs amputated after developing gangrene from frostbite induced while trapping one winter. The doctor cut off his first leg when the former quarry and sawmill operator was 91, the second leg 10 months later. He died in 1938 at age 98. Hort and Rex were the second and eighth of his 13 children.

Rex was 60 when Koestner bought his land. Rex had moved back to the old Jeremy homestead sometime after his wife was killed in a cookstove explosion and fire in the late 1930s. The couple had lived in North Dakota, where Rex operated a lumberyard.

Rex, the river rat, and Don the artist, gradually became friends. The two men beachcombed with a small, flat-bottomed boat that Koestner had bought; Rex played the mentoring role. They explored the sandbars for drift lumber caught on the banks, dragged found material to the boat, and pulled it to the shore with a 10-foot "pick pole" with a spike on the end.

To Koestner's amazement, the river carried endless treasures down the river from St. Paul. Building material included old bridge timbers and railroad ties, and occasionally a sheet of plywood that, if retrieved from the sandbars soon enough, was usable.

"A good beachcomber checks the river often," Rex said.

The distance from the shore to the top of Koestner's bluff was about 35 feet, the incline steep but climbable. One piece of drift lumber Koestner dragged ashore was a creosoted plank three feet long, two feet wide, and eight inches thick—a foundation post for the cabin. He got it up the bank end over end. He moved heavier timbers up the bluff from tree to tree, using a block and tackle with a 15-foot rope. Both Hort and Rex Jeremy were impressed by the wiry young artist's determination.

Koestner's building experience was limited to watching his father and brother-in-law add a room to his sister's home. Now, as he drove his cab around the burgeoning Minneapolis suburbs of Richfield and Bloomington, he observed new house construction for tips on laying floor joists and framing walls and roofs. His curiosity and common sense, combined with his mechanical aptitude and memory for detail, enabled him to apply what he observed. He became not a master of the building trades but a lifelong journeyman. The skills and savvy were in his blood.

He devoted the summer of 1951 to building his cabin, first

laying a foundation of wood posts the eight inches or so to bedrock. He creosoted the posts before putting them in the ground, even though Rex thought this was not necessary.

"Even the way they are, they'll last 10 years," Rex said. "And by that time you'll want to get married, and the old lady will make you move to the city."

Building his own structure with hand tools fostered in Koestner a profound sense of independence. He cut every board with a handsaw—tiring work with freshly milled lumber, let alone age-hardened wood. Koestner soon learned that a sharpened saw cuts more easily than a dull one. Building the cabin literally with his own hands provided him insight into home ownership that few come to know. "Home" was not an abstraction or turnkey passage into a ready-made box of rooms. Building his house from the ground up, he felt the structure gain rigidity through his own effort. Once the walls were up, he added a roof, tar-papered and shingled it to keep out rain, and installed the salvaged windows and door.

To the outside of the framing, Koestner nailed boards from the $40-takes-all sale. He covered these with a layer of waterproof sheeting—fancy roll goods, like roofing paper but imprinted with a red-brick pattern. On the inside walls and ceiling he applied fiber wallboard. He obtained all of the wallboard, advertised in the newspaper, for $20. The subflooring was laid with rough boards. On top he put a layer of 30-pound felt paper, then a thick layer of newspapers and a second layer of felt. Over that he nailed used tongue and groove boards.

Koestner's completed cabin (14-by-22-feet) was twice the size of Thoreau's ("ten feet wide by fifteen long"), but like Thoreau, Koestner kept a careful record of his building expenses. When it was done, with four walls and a roof, plus an old coal-burning space heater bought for $7 and converted to burn wood, Koestner had spent $300 out of pocket. (In comparison, in the 1950s a new, suburban three-bedroom rambler with 1,000 square feet of living space cost about $10,000, including a small lot.) Taking into consideration the change in the dollar's buying power over the course of a century, Koestner's total cash outlay for his cabin was comparable to Thoreau's $28. To Koestner, it was a measure of his achievement, proof he could live cheaply as well as simply.

Cabin furnishings included the woodstove and an old icebox. Water for cooking and washing was held in a washtub mounted on a stand. A spigot near the bottom allowed him to conveniently fill his cooking pot.

Initially, Koestner planned to live without electricity. Then he learned from Hort Jeremy that the Rural Electrification Administration (REA) would bring in a power line for a one-time service deposit of $5. REA was a federal "New Deal" program organized by the Department of Agriculture in 1935 to bring electricity to rural areas. Koestner signed up for the program, and within days an REA crew was on his property blasting holes to set five poles in the limestone rock of the bluff. It took them a week to finish the job. Meanwhile, Koestner bought a manual on how to install electric wiring. Soon he had electric lights and outlets for a radio and hot plate.

"The best bargain I ever got for five bucks," he said.

Koestner moved into his cabin the day after Labor Day 1951. Now, at last, he had his weekdays to paint, except for the time cutting and stacking firewood and doing routine household chores. But to his amazement, when the turning leaves called him as a painter to nature's most glorious season, he suddenly felt overwhelmed, unprepared to utilize the subject matter all around him. He walked through the woods wondering what to paint. He asked himself, "Do I belong here? Should I be here at all?"

In mid-October an unexpected snowstorm put an end to fall

colors and Koestner's doubts. He had to cut firewood because he hadn't yet stockpiled enough for the winter. Since the power company had cut down a number of trees while installing lines to the cabin, he had an ample supply. He used a one-man crosscut saw to cut the felled trees into stove lengths. He initially cut enough wood for a three-to-four-day supply, then maintained it with an after-breakfast routine of cutting, splitting, and stacking firewood for an hour.

Heating the cabin was another challenge. He had never operated a woodstove, and he learned by trial and error which variety of wood burned fast and which burned slowly and steadily. A woodstove, unlike a central heating system, is essentially a space heater. The trick was to learn how to regulate the heat so that during waking hours the temperature stayed at a comfortable 65 to 75 degrees F. Part of that challenge was to select the right wood and load it in the right amount. Pine makes a fast, hot fire but lasts a shorter time than birch, which burns more slowly—though not as slowly as oak and hickory, which give the most even heat. Koestner acquired a feel for this over time. On one occasion, the stovepipe got red hot and nearly ignited the ceiling.

Koestner also learned that the heating value of wood increased as it dried. The drier the wood, the easier it was for him to tend and regulate the stove's heat. Green wood, freshly cut from his woods, was so high in water content that it took six months or more to season thoroughly. He had to plan ahead and stockpile his fuel. That first winter, Koestner learned that the hungry stove ate an hour's worth of woodcutting in just 24 hours. He took the precaution of stockpiling more, to cover himself in the event of a storm or sickness. He burned between three and four cords of firewood during the winter. (A cord measures four feet by four feet by eight feet.)

Koestner's water source was the Mississippi River and a rain barrel. The well Hort Jeremy mentioned did exist, but someone had filled much of it with stones and other debris. Hort, qualifying his earlier promise of help, suggested they address the problem "at a later time." Meanwhile, Koestner carried water from the river up the bluff in a bucket and boiled it for drinking. That winter, he chopped a hole through the river ice with a hatchet to get water. When the ice got too thick to penetrate, he melted snow on his woodstove. Beginning that winter, he took stand-up baths in his kitchen. His toilet was an outhouse.

Painting kept Koestner occupied during that first winter. He got his art-school friend Chuck Gravem to model for him in motorcycling attire. He first did a drawing, then a life-size, full-figure oil portrait. The painting style he emulated was that of Hans Holbein the Younger, a sixteenth-century German painter known for bold, honest portraits of aristocrats and scholars. The ambitious project took Koestner two months to complete but got him involved in painting again.

Koestner also received a commission from his Uncle Frank in Becker to do a painting for his parish, St. Mary's Catholic Church. The project, a depiction of Jesus and his disciples for the church's nursery, was to illustrate the biblical quotation: "Suffer the little children to come unto me." He posed for the disciples himself, wrapped in a sheet to simulate biblical dress. One morning as he posed before a mirror, Rex walked in on him, and he had to quickly explain what he was doing. The painting turned out "fairly well," though artist friends told him that all the heads, except that of Jesus, looked like Don.

Finding female models posed a problem for a shy, frugal artist living in the country. It occurred to Koestner that his neighbor Leland (Lee) Lyon, a blacksmith, might be able to fabricate a model from metal in his shop—perhaps a mannequin with rotating elbow, hip, and knee joints and a bendable neck so he could easily mold the figure into various positions. He sought out the blacksmith in the back of his shop.

"Lee, can you help me make a woman?" he blurted, knowing that would get a rise out of Lyon.

Koestner described his project in more detail and the good-natured blacksmith said he'd give it a try. Regrettably, the metal dummy he constructed, once padded and clothed (by fellow painter Richard Lack's wife, Katherine, and dubbed "Marilyn" by friends), turned out to have masculine proportions and was set aside as a failed experiment.

Nothing can come out of an artist that is not in the man.
H. L. Mencken

Roots

KOESTNER'S FIRST WINTER IN NININGER tested his resolve. Outside temperatures were often below zero for days at a time, requiring him to get up during the night to add fuel to the stove. He experienced some uneasiness but gradually adjusted to his solitude.

On weekends he continued to drive a cab in the city, staying overnight with his parents in Bloomington. During his absence, the cabin became an icebox. Rex Jeremy came in on Sunday afternoons and lit a fire, so that when Koestner returned in the evening his cabin was warm. Koestner brought with him a week's groceries (some for Rex) and a box of clean laundry. These he hauled the half-mile to his cabin on an orange crate he'd attached to a sled. Rex's dog, Bosco, awaited his arrival and trotted behind the sled to the cabin.

Lee Lyon, who lived next to the road, was sympathetic to Koestner and let him park his car by the blacksmith shop. During the week the car sat idle, but on Friday mornings Lyon connected its head-bolt heater to his power source so that the engine would start when Koestner needed to leave for the city. Lyon had volunteered this service without Koestner's asking.

That winter—1952—Koestner discovered a design/engineering flaw in his home. The cabin rested on posts, with a crawl space beneath that exposed the floor to the cold. As a result, the inside temperature of the walls near the ceiling reached 80 degrees F., but only 55 on the floor. The following spring, Koestner temporarily enclosed the foundation with scraps of wood and several heavy-duty grain doors salvaged from the river. The huge doors made of plywood, with wood boards fastened on one side, were too cumbersome to move up the embankment by hand—or even with block and tackle. So Koestner floated the doors a quarter mile downriver beyond his property to the landing at Walt's Cave and loaded them on his trailer.

The crudely enclosed crawl space inspired an innovation. Koestner built a 2-by-3-foot brick enclosure beneath his floor, making it accessible with a 15-by-24-inch trapdoor. This became his cooler, replacing the icebox. The temperature in the box held to about 60 degrees F. during the summer. It kept a quart of milk or package of lunch meat fairly cool, though he had to consume the products within two days. In winter, the below-floor cooler performed exceptionally well, keeping food at a usable temperature even when the cabin temperature dropped below freezing— as it did on the weekends he was in the city.

The following summer, 1953, Koestner built a stone foundation. He made mortar mix with sand obtained on an island in the river. On his first trip back to shore, his leaky, overloaded boat began to sink, and he had to shovel out most of what he'd collected. He carried the sand he was able to salvage up the embankment by bucket. Building the stone foundation took several months.

That summer, Koestner enlisted Hort (Captain) Jeremy's help in restoring the old well. Hauling water out of the river and up the bluff by the bucketful was tiresome and time-consuming, so he had used water sparingly—usually only two pails a day. When Hort came around one day and asked about the well, Koestner told him that someone had filled it with rocks.

"Aw, that's probably just a plug in there," Hort said. "I bet I'll be able to get water for you."

Hort, then 70, built a tripod out of box-elder saplings. He next devised a winch on a wooden cylinder to which he added a wooden crank. Koestner helped him build the apparatus. The captain borrowed 100 feet of cable from operators he knew at the Hastings dam and also obtained a chunk of large iron pipe that he could fill with stones. Neighbor Lee Lyon welded a cap on the bottom and a U-bolt on the top so they could attach the cable.

Koestner dropped the weighted pipe like a battering ram, then the two men cranked it back up for another blow. In a short time, Hort's improvised rock-buster broke through the debris and dropped to the bottom of what originally had been a 110-foot well. Because of rocks, there was only about 2½ feet of water at the bottom—but it was fresh water.

Next they exchanged the battering ram and cable for a five-foot-long, sheet-metal downspout and lengths of heavy rope. The experienced river man spliced rather than knotted the rope. Hort attached a leather flap on the bottom of the downspout so that it would open to admit water at the bottom of the well and then close to contain the water as the metal tube was winched up. Two

full downspouts filled a bucket. Koestner used the home-engi-
neered apparatus for several years, then installed a hand pump on
a pipe that reached to the well's bottom. With his water supply a
bit easier to access, he began bathing (summers) in a claw-foot
tub set behind the cabin. He waited for the sun to raise the temperature of the six inches or so of well water he had poured into
the tub, then at bath time added a teakettle of boiling water.

—⟋⟍⟍—

IN AN ERA OF RAMPANT CHANGE and rampant consumerism,
Koestner was a nonconformist. For him, getting by represented
the reward of time more than the denial of goods. His friends and
associates admired his tenacity, discipline, and independence.

Locally, Koestner acquired an identity as the "artist of
Nininger." He didn't invite attention, but his unpretentious, work-
manlike approach to his art, his industriousness as it related to
scavenging and cabin building, his openness and respectfulness,
and his spartan lifestyle—all wore well with his rural community.
His friendship with Rex Jeremy deepened, and Rex took it upon
himself occasionally to bring neighbors to the cabin to show them
what Koestner was painting. Whether a human likeness, landscape, or still life, Rex called the work in progress a "portrait."

Koestner's woodland surroundings were reminiscent of the
nineteenth-century landscape paintings he admired. Sometimes
cows grazed outside his kitchen window. These were owned by
farmer and town-board supervisor Leo Conzemius, who lived several miles away. One spring morning Koestner noticed a string of
"stuff" hanging beneath the tail of one of the cows. As a city boy,
he didn't know what it was and went to a neighbor to telephone
Conzemius, who immediately understood what the artist had
seen—placenta, or afterbirth. It signaled to Conzemius that there
was a newborn calf somewhere in the tall pasture grass. He came

right over, found the calf—which was healthy and already licked clean—and got it back to its mother.

The winter of 1953-54, Koestner switched from weekend cab driving to a more lucrative weekday schedule to save money for a four-month European bike trip he and Cliff Moen had planned for the following summer. His arrangement with Richfield Cab owner Ellsworth (Pete) Peterson had been a boon. He appreciated his employer's willingness to let him work only on weekends over the previous three years. At the time they made the earlier agreement, Koestner had told Peterson that if he became shorthanded during the week he would come in to help. In one such emergency, Peterson had tried to reach him on a Monday morning by telegram as Koestner had no phone. Koestner didn't find the telegram in his mailbox until the following Friday night. It wasn't his habit to check for mail during the week.

In April 1954, Koestner and Moen left for Quebec in Koestner's 1939 Chrysler. Koestner had saved $250 for the trip driving cab full time the previous winter. He offered Rex the use of his cabin while he was gone, and Rex appreciated the opportunity to live independently of his brother, Hort. Rex planned to build a cabin of his own in the fall, and while living in Koestner's cabin to collect lumber from the river and other sources.

The two Europe-bound artists camped as they traveled east, except in Quebec where it was so cold and wet they rented a hotel room for $3. To offset that luxury, Koestner bought two fresh eggs for breakfast the next morning, bored a small hole in one end and sucked out the insides—a practice Koestner (but not Moen) continued in Europe. Before boarding their ship, Koestner parked his car in a farmer's field, then removed the license plates and left them with the Canadian customs department. The voyage up the St. Lawrence River from Quebec and across the Atlantic to the French coast on the British liner *Sythia* took five days.

At the port of Le Havre, Koestner and Moen bought bicycles for $50 apiece, a cash outlay cutting severely into their travel budget. Though they thought they had brought minimum gear, they soon realized that their heavily loaded bikes were too hard to steer. Keeping only bedrolls, pup tents, one change of clothes, and a single mess kit, they knocked on a French farmer's door and gave him a windfall of useful items.

Much of Europe was still recovering from World War II, and the cyclists met with little automobile traffic. Their 100-mile ride to Paris, some of it following the Seine River, took three days. Near the end of the first day, they bought a bottle of wine and a loaf of bread and celebrated in an orchard alongside the road. The next morning they awoke to find their bikes, parked on the riverbank, half-submerged from heavy rains. They spent four days in Paris, visiting the Louvre several times and seeing other museums, then pedaled south to Toulouse (via Orleans, Tours, La Rochelle, and Bordeaux), doing pen-and-wash sketches almost every day. They often biked in a mist, during what was later determined to be the rainiest summer in Europe in 73 years.

After visiting Toulouse, the pair biked east through France and northern Italy. In a Florence museum, Koestner saw what he thought were exceptional oil sketches. They were small sketches done on location rather than in a studio, perhaps in an hour or two. What these artists had succeeded in capturing on canvas, Koestner thought, was fleeting and immediate. Two of the nineteenth-century French painters Koestner admired—Camille Corot and Claude Monet—worked in this style. He had seen their works in several American museum collections and felt a kinship. Now, seeing their oil sketches, he decided to abandon his pen and wash sketching and, when he returned home, do oil sketches in the field.

From Italy, Koestner and Moen biked through Austria and into Germany as far as Frankfurt. There they sold their bicycles for $15 each and hitchhiked north through Belgium and Holland, then ferried across the English Channel to spend a week in London.

Travel on a shoestring can test even the best of friends, and this pair was no exception. As they left Paris early in the trip, Koestner suggested they visit Barbizon, a village a few miles southeast of Paris, where a number of well-known nineteenth-century landscape painters, including Corot and Jean-Francois Millet, had worked. Moen vetoed the idea because it departed from their travel plan. Koestner was irked, but he acquiesced. Later, in Germany, Moen suggested they detour to Wittenberg, the city where in 1517 Martin Luther posted his 95 theses on the door of Castle Church, fueling the Reformation. Koestner refused: "No Barbizon, no Wittenberg."

Their disagreements underscored a difference in the goals of the two strong-willed artists. Koestner was in Europe to visit as many museums and famous landscape painting sites as their timetable and budget allowed; he also wanted to absorb the countryside. For him, the trip was about sketching and seeing art. But Moen, a lean six-footer with long legs, wished to cover as much ground and see as many cities as possible. He loved to travel, and he was competitive, once racing ahead of his partner, then waiting for him several miles down the road. When Koestner caught up, he blithely pedaled by. For the most part, the two friends enjoyed conversation pedaling beside each other, their brains, Moen said, "oxygenated to the full from our exertions." Sometimes, they became so lost in their exuberant talk that they held up traffic on the narrow roads. They returned to Quebec from Liverpool and arrived home in August.

Koestner was spiritually enriched from seeing so much art and experiencing the European countryside he had admired in museum landscape paintings. But he was weary from his four-month adventure. He returned to a tightly sealed cabin that, on his opening of the door, smelled like a garbage pit. It was immediately clear to him that Rex, who had left a note saying he was with his daughter for a week, had not emptied the wastewater bucket for some time. Nor had he removed the storm windows and put on screens to provide ventilation during the summer months.

Too tired to deal with any of it, Koestner loaded his bedroll and painting gear into the boat and camped overnight on an island in the river. He was so discouraged by the mess that he found himself wondering whether he wanted to live there at all. Camping that night under a black sky alive with stars, listening to the river's flow, he decided he had made the right choice.

Rex started building his own cabin in September, then fell off the roof and broke his collarbone. The injury slowed construction for more than a week. During that period, Koestner gave Rex his bed and slept on the floor. In exchange, Rex bought the groceries and got up during the night to add wood to the fire. That fall, Koestner and Dick Sabol, another art-school friend, finished most of Rex's roofing.

As Koestner's third winter in Nininger approached, he began a painting of a large elm tree with silver moonlight passing through its branches. The subject was the same elm whose young roots had once entwined Alexander Jeremy's amputated leg.

Leap Year

ALTHOUGH DON KOESTNER WAS MORE SOLITARY than communal, old art-school friends occasionally appeared on his doorstep. In 1953, Chuck Gravem bought a small parcel of land nearby—a tax sale on additional property owned by Rex Jeremy. Gravem built a small cabin, and occasionally spent time there, mainly to enjoy the river. The two artists had China, as well as art, in common. Koestner served in China during World War II, and Gravem lived there before the war as the child of American missionaries. Gravem sold his Nininger property in 1954, while Koestner and Cliff Moen were in Europe.

In June 1955, Vince and Joyce Houser Peterson—both former

MSA students—dropped in on Koestner and ended up staying the summer. Koestner had dated Joyce Houser in art school, and sometime after settling in Nininger he proposed marriage to her. Though seeking solitude, he said, "I never intended to live a hermit's life." When Joyce declined, he was disappointed. When Vince and Joyce later announced their marriage plans, Koestner was devastated. But with Chuck Gravem's advice not to hold a grudge, he got over it. Since graduation from art school, Vince had worked as a hospital orderly but quit his job to take the summer off before moving to Joyce's hometown in Pennsylvania. During a visit with Koestner three years earlier, Peterson built a roof over the foundation of the original Jeremy family homestead and camped there for a few weeks. Now Vince and Joyce set up temporary residence in the roofed-over hole.

During this period, Koestner swapped his 1939 Chrysler for a 1939 International panel truck. The trade cost him $40 out of pocket. He called the small truck his "Bambi wagon" because of its former use for local bread delivery by a bakery of that name. Koestner saw it as an ideal vehicle for sketching trips around Nininger and the outer ring of the Twin Cities metro area as well as for camping. The truck had a swivel driver's seat and panel doors that folded back for easy access. Its windshield was plate glass measuring about 3-by-4 feet—an ideal picture window. Remaining in the parked truck, Koestner could view subjects straight ahead or turn left or right to make sketches of what he could see through the door openings.

Bambi doubled as a pack mule when Koestner added a "stone room" to his cabin. His discovery of discarded flagstones left from an airport construction project inspired the addition. These flagstones became the stone room's floor. He also found red bricks from a torn-down telephone company building in Bloomington, dumped to fill an oversized hole dug for a church expansion project. Koestner thought that a waste of good brick so helped himself to several loads. He collected enough for two fireplaces and two chimneys—one for himself and one for Rex Jeremy. And finally, for building the walls that flanked the fireplace, he rescued a pile of eight-inch granite blocks that once lay between streetcar tracks later torn up on a south Minneapolis street.

Geared low for in-town deliveries, Bambi had a top speed of 30 miles per hour. One Friday evening, Koestner headed north on Minnesota 55 for his weekend of cab driving. Coming south was a highway patrol car. As the officer approached Koestner, he yelled out his window, "Go *faster!*" Koestner looked in his rearview mirror and saw a long line of cars behind him. He pulled over on the shoulder, vowing to drive to and from the Twin Cities only on available county roads. He often traveled back roads at night—moonlit nights, because the slow-moving truck seldom generated enough power to run the headlights. Fall turned to winter, and he postponed construction of the addition until the following summer.

The granite blocks salvaged from the Minneapolis street reconstruction comprised the stone room's east and west walls. The blocks were stacked to waist level, and above them he nailed oak panels from the interior of the Bambi wagon. The floor was laid with yellow-gray flagstone salvaged from the airport project. Koestner first positioned the stones on the subfloor and marked each one, then removed them to pour a base of concrete. Art-school friend Dick Sabol helped lay the flagstones.

The addition's south wall was primarily a massive red-brick fireplace, its mantel a piece of rough-sawn timber Koestner had pulled from the river years earlier and saved for future use. Rex Jeremy built the fireplace, first chipping mortar off the old bricks with a brick hammer and neatly stacking them near the work site. Now 65 years of age, he still enjoyed manual labor, especially masonry work. The payment for his labor was a load of bricks provided for his own fireplace and chimney, plus Koestner's pancake breakfasts. The two men were a model of cooperation.

Once the fireplace project was under way, Bambi became the work crew's Gunga Din, carting the water needed for masonry. Koestner and Rex Jeremy filled a 50-gallon drum at the boat landing and slowly hauled it up hill to the work site. On this assignment, balance was more important than speed.

—⚡—

THROUGH THE 1950s Koestner's painting steadily improved. Painting as often as he did contributed to his growth, but supporting that was his serious study of museum collections. "I think the biggest influence on my work were the trips I took with a conscious desire to learn from other painters," he said. Museum visits allowed him to examine brushstroke details, glazes, and the color and value nuances he sought to understand. Over time, he began to recognize techniques and effects that he could try in his own paintings.

"I started out being influenced by Holbein," he said. "A far cry from my turning out to be an impressionist."

While some artists considered Holbein's work overly detailed, even "photographic," Koestner did not: "What drew me to him was the beautiful simplicity of his design and drawing."

Studying Monet's paintings at the Art Institute of Chicago, Koestner recognized a tendency in his own work to be too literal, and he began to soften his edges. Looking at Vermeer's work made him pay more attention to his compositional design. In examining works of Hudson River School painters Asher B. Durand and Albert Bierstadt, he saw how their wide value range—virtually black to white—"put punch in their paintings."

On museum trips, Koestner often traveled back roads, doing

oil sketches along the way. In the summer of 1955 he visited museums in Washington, D.C., exploring the Blue Ridge Mountains en route. On this trip he traveled with his cousin, Art Koestner—in Art's 1951 Pontiac. Art was four years older than Don, and the two sometimes got together for a few beers at the end of Don's Saturday-night cab-driving shift in the city. Intelligent and resourceful, Art had attended radio school in Chicago, then learned to fly small aircraft—both on the GI Bill. He knew nothing about art but was open to new experiences. He was the only cousin who respected Don's fascination with landscape painting, though he didn't consider it a serious vocation. Looking across a panoramic valley that his cousin was sketching, Art said, "I never thought doing nothing could be so interesting."

Living in Nininger, Koestner had time to reflect—not only about art, but about nature, religion, and life in general. He was inquisitive and read a good deal. Reading tired his eyes, however, so he was selective about what he picked up. His library at the time included scores of books on art and artists, philosophy, fiction, and poetry. For news and commentary, he listened almost exclusively to KUOM, the University of Minnesota radio station. Television was new and of no interest to him. Other than reading *TIME* magazine while waiting for customers in his cab driving years, he read magazines only rarely. He regarded most of that material as noise intruding on his quiet, focused life.

Koestner wrote two letters to Cliff Moen in March and July 1956 (saved by Moen) providing insights into his life in Nininger. At the time, Moen was prospecting for uranium in the West, moving from one site to another. He collected his mail by general delivery. Koestner's 10- and 12-page letters, written with a legible but fast-moving left hand, capture a torrent of thought and opinion.

In one letter to Moen, Koestner vented his frustration with a magazine article describing nineteenth-century impressionist painters as revolting against traditional painting:

> Their revolt was not against the use of visible form as valid artistic expression, but merely against the decadent and entrenched academy in France. In the solidity and quality of their work they were going back [to traditional roots] for inspiration. No one studied the masters more than Degas, Renoir, Monet, and others loosely labeled as Impressionists. Renoir was closer to Rubens than to his contemporary French academy, and Degas advocated copying Holbein as the best means to learn draftsmanship, and there are analogies between Van Gogh and Rembrandt. Yet for some curious reason the Impressionists have been the excuse for every incompetent brush-wielder from Cezanne on down to destroy the essential communicability of the art of painting. I include Cezanne for I believe he is largely overrated.

Koestner also described painting projects he had under way. These included several portraits, plus four landscapes he painted outdoors on small gesso panels, then in the studio on fairly large canvases—"but in the more direct and intense method I used on the gesso panels." Of the four, he says, "One is a flop; two I'm not yet certain of; but one I think good—at least on my level. This stepped-up painting production has necessitated, alas, [more] time spent in grinding paint and preparing canvases."

Koestner also questioned his progress as a painter: "Always in the background are misgivings about the worth of what I do. I don't feel that I have 'found' myself yet."

In the second letter to Moen, Koestner described his wine-making efforts in a paragraph that smacked of Steinbeck's *Cannery Row*: "To answer your inquiry about my wine. It remained too sweet, but by happy coincidence Rex's turned out too sour, so we mixed the two together and—presto—we have some good wine . . . Just this week I made a tour of the junk shop with Rex, and we came upon a dandy little wine press and a five-gallon wine keg, so we are all set for the next wild grape harvest."

In this letter, Koestner rationalizes an upcoming road trip, telling Moen he had questioned the wisdom of taking another trip when he could be at home painting: "In the end, I realized that such a trip would do me good even if I don't paint as much as I might right here. In fact, I am looking forward to it more now as a time for that necessary introspection than for actual production."

In early July 1956, Koestner set off on a two-month museum and sketching trip to the East coast, this time traveling alone. Starting out from Nininger, he took country roads to Chicago, then continued east to visit museums in Detroit, Toledo, Buffalo, Cleveland, Boston, Washington, D.C., Baltimore, Philadelphia, and New York. His transportation was a 20-year-old Pontiac sedan he bought from a fellow cabbie for $60. To prepare for the trip, he removed the car's front bench seat and replaced it with a single bucket seat from Rex's junked Ford. He thereby made space on the right side of the car for a full-length bed. (The former bench seat became a couch for the cabin.) For oil sketching he prepared 30 or more gesso panels cut to 8-by-10-inch and 10-by-12-inch sizes. To keep them dust free and supported after painting on them, he constructed a box with grooves on two sides. On the road he ate dried and canned food purchased during the winter with his cab-driving income. He spent only $200 on the two-month journey. But on his return he decided that in the future he would restrict the areas he sketched on cross-country trips. There simply was too much beauty to absorb.

Excerpts from his journal offer a glimpse of his road experience—what he observed and what he learned:

July 14: At fine campsite at Indiana Dunes State Park (cost 72 cents). Had a cold shower and washed clothes. This forest of fine oaks quite a contrast from the night in a cheap, hot and dirty hotel off Clark Street in Chicago ($1.75, including bedbugs). Made two visits to Chicago Art Institute, and have been helped by them, I think. I was again made aware of the necessity for me of these periodic visits to see good paintings. Really "saw" [painter George] Inness for the first time and was much impressed.

July 17: Yesterday, spent four or five hours in Detroit Museum. Concentrated on my preference this time for American and Impressionist painters. Appreciated John Sloan's [paintings]. Also Eastman Johnson and other Americans who I know little about. Also liked seeing Rubens, Titian, and especially Bruegel.

July 18: Spent three hours in the Toledo Museum this morning, again much impressed by the quality of [the] Toledo collection. Particularly liked a fine example of Inness' *After a Spring Shower.*

Aug. 17: Back on the road again after three weeks in NYC. Enjoyed the peaceful quiet of sitting across the road from a pasture to paint old tree in afternoon—could see the far bank of the Hudson [River] from my position.

Aug. 19: Painted stream in the Catskills yesterday morning. Drove yesterday afternoon through a gray misty landscape. Rained toward evening and most of the night. This morning I backtracked about five miles to paint old deserted house which I had spotted before camping last night.

Aug. 23: Buffalo: The Albright Gallery. Fine Eakins, Millet, Sargent. Spent day on deserted beach road overlooking the lake [Erie]. Painted coast in evening; took notes of fine moonrise.

Aug. 25: Drove to Toledo in afternoon, down same road I traveled in July. Toledo Museum impressed me as usual. . . . I suspected that perhaps I had overestimated Inness' *Spring Shower*, but no. I still consider it one of the finest landscapes I've ever seen. Also like [Albert] Ryder's small scene. The two have much the same mysticism (nebulous, misty shapes). Liked also Inness' *Sunset 1891*. It is done in very thick pigments.

Aug. 28: Should be in Rochester [Minnesota] tomorrow evening if the car holds out.

—m—

DURING THE WINTER OF 1956-57, Koestner saw a Monet show at the Art Institute of Chicago, a museum he tried to visit at least once a year because of its exceptional collections. The artists he admired worked in varying styles, some more realistic or romantic or impressionistic than others, but all had similar attributes. All drew figures and objects well. All designed well. Their works often evoked a kind of simplicity and truthfulness about nature. But in Monet, particularly, Koestner saw what he called a "soft poetry." He began to see Monet in a new way—and impressionism as a style to emulate.

Though Koestner worked diligently, he found gauging his progress difficult. One painting experience, however, stood out as a turning point. In midsummer 1957 he painted a sunrise view of the St. Paul Cathedral from the High Bridge, built in the late 1800s to carry horse-drawn traffic across the Mississippi River to a growing west St. Paul neighborhood called Cherokee Heights (near the artist's childhood home). Until this time, he had a tendency to paint in a fairly dark tonal range. But when he walked back to his car at the end of this session and viewed the scene again, he noticed how light the cathedral was compared to the nearby trees. He suddenly knew he had made the painting too dark by keying the value to the foreground rather than to the distant subject. He lightened the painting "by about half" and was amazed at the improvement.

That year, 1958, Koestner sold a piece of his Nininger property to Cliff Moen, who, recently married, built a house on it the next year. Moen had met his wife, Barbara Stratton, at a YMCA dance in Minneapolis he and Koestner had attended, looking for girls they could date. The dance was held in a large meeting room, the men standing in a ring while the women circled inside the ring. Barbara, a school librarian from Springfield, Massachusetts, described what happened next: "When the girls were signaled to stop, whoever they stood in front of, they were obliged to talk to—and that's how I met Cliff." Don drove each of them home from the dance. A year after their marriage, Koestner teased Moen, "Well, it looks like it's working out; maybe I should try and find someone."

Koestner began teaching an art group, the Palette Club in Hastings, one evening a week. The club's membership of men and women had discovered him through Harry Benjamin, president of the local phone company, who told them about "an artist living in the woods." Impressed with Koestner's dedication and talent, club members immediately took to him. He, in turn, enjoyed the social contact as much as the teaching opportunity. Club members Karen Olson and Luann Stoffel, influential in the community, boosted his confidence and gave him visibility. They set the stage for future art shows in Hastings. Stoffel (later a three-term mayor of Hastings) was president of the Hastings Women's Club. In a meeting with a group from another Mississippi River town— Red Wing—she arranged a second teaching opportunity for Koestner. In the fall of 1959, he began to teach three adult classes one day a week with the Red Wing Art History Club. The income—$30 for the day—was enough to live on for a week and allowed him to give up his cab driving. He promised the owner, Pete Peterson, he would still drive on occasion if needed.

That December, Koestner visited Chicago to see Monet's paintings—particularly his later works—again. More atmospheric than his earlier works, these depictions viewed nature "from a distance and you couldn't see any details," according to Koestner. Looking closely at Monet's brush strokes and palette, Koestner observed his use of spots of color in juxtaposition with others— and how the eye mixed them. This "broken color" method of replicating the effects of light and color in nature gave Monet's paintings both the impression of reality and the poetic softness Koestner admired. He had looked at these paintings many times before, but suddenly he understood what he was seeing. This revelation was another turning point.

After nearly a decade of painting, Koestner attributed the breakthrough in his ability as a painter to his recent insights on Monet. His students in the Palette Club had a different view. They linked Koestner's blossoming to his meeting a petite young woman from Maiden Rock, Wisconsin—Fern Bolin.

—◊◊◊—

ELIZABETH FERN BOLIN GREW UP NEAR LAKE PEPIN, a widening in the Mississippi River below Red Wing—but on the Wisconsin side. Born June 1, 1934, she was the oldest of eight children in a family that went back several generations in Pierce County. Her paternal great-grandfather, Shubel Bolin, had come from Terre Haute, Indiana in the 1850s and homesteaded several hundred acres. The Bolins were Engish. Fern's mother, Agnes Louise Burridge, was born in Newfoundland and also was of English descent. Agnes's parents, Samuel and Ella, moved to Pierce County in the 1920s. For a time, they and a partner operated a sand mine in Maiden Rock. Agnes was just 16 when she married Francis Bolin and 17 when Fern was born. The marriage didn't last, and Fern's father moved out when Fern was in fourth grade.

Agnes, though attractive, was shy and insecure. After her husband left, she shunned being in public. Fern, at age nine, became the family's shopper and fixer. Though small for her age, she was outgoing, determined, and responsible. Her mother taught her to "squeeze every penny" before it left her fingers.

Fern was raised in a fundamentalist Christian environment. The worshippers, unaffiliated with any church, met in each other's homes and called themselves "the Faith." One person in the group volunteered as minister and traveled to various home gatherings to lead services.

Fern seldom dated; her spare time was committed to the care of her seven younger siblings. The youngest two were the children of Agnes and her second husband, Everett, Francis Bolin's brother. The older children avoided him because of his temper and unreasonable demands. Fern helped her five younger sisters and two brothers with their homework, sewed dresses for the girls, disciplined the boys when they were out of line, and read to them all at bedtime. She occasionally made fudge, cautioning them to be careful about the foods they consumed. "You are what you eat," she said. She also had a saying about homework and household chores: "If anything is worth doing, it's worth doing well." Years later, when her youngest sister applied for nurse's training, Fern lent her the money for her first year's expenses (later repaid). Self-reliance was a trademark of the Bolin children.

Fern was a straight-A student at Red Wing High School, where she also won top honors for her artwork. Following graduation, she worked for four years at the local Ben Franklin store, then was employed by the Chalet Studio, a local photo shop. Fern's new employer trained her in darkroom work, photo retouching, and photo coloring.

Fern met Don at a show of his work in Red Wing and was impressed by his ability. She had previously attended art workshops in "modern painting" and had low regard for it. When she saw a Koestner still life, her estimate of his talent leaped. The flaming candles in his painting seemed so real, she said, "I thought I could blow them out." A month later, in January 1960, at the urging of her landlady, Fern joined Koestner's Red Wing painting class. In talking with him, she immediately sensed "he knew what he was talking about." She admired his intensity and sincerity and enjoyed his droll sense of humor.

"Fern was talkative and friendly," Koestner remembers. He asked her whether she'd like to have dinner with him the next week before class. On February 29 they had their first date, dinner at Nybo's Restaurant in Red Wing. Through the meal and over coffee and hot chocolate, Fern mostly listened and Don talked.

"A lot," Fern said. "I mean he had been alone for quite awhile."

Don expected they'd then go to the class, "and that would be it." But February 29 being Leap Year Day—the one day every four years when the ancient rules of courtship empowered women— Fern chose not to drive to class and required that Don take her home. After class, he suggested they go to Nybo's again and have a cup of coffee and a piece of pie. They talked until midnight.

More dates followed, and by the end of April the courtship was serious. That spring, Koestner invited Fern to his cabin for dinner. Not wanting to risk any semblance of impropriety, he also invited Howard and Dolly Hyde, an older couple from Red Wing whom Fern considered her second parents.

Don's friend and now neighbor, Cliff Moen, advised against a spring timetable for Fern's first visit because of the ankle-deep mud on their half-mile road.

"She'll never come back," he predicted.

Koestner disregarded Moen's counsel. He thought it better that Fern experience his place "warts and all." Warts included not only the mud but also his cabin's lack of running water and indoor toilet.

Fern was not in the least discouraged. She was a small-town girl who had experienced rustic conditions growing up. She and her companions found the cabin charming and its river overlook beautiful. Fern had lived near the river all her life—once on a farm overlooking Lake Pepin—and the setting felt like home. Dinner was hot dogs roasted in the stone-room's fireplace.

Also that April, the Palette Club group sponsored a show of Koestner's paintings at the Hastings Public Library. An article in the *St. Paul Pioneer Press* attracted an appreciative audience— "Artist's Reward Not Gold Alone" the headline read—and Koestner earned $400 in sales. A windfall, considering his average monthly income was $135. He immediately hired Lee Lyon to overhaul the high-mileage engine of his latest automobile—a 1951 Plymouth bought for $100.

Don and Fern married in St. Paul on June 30, 1960, before a justice of the peace with an office on University Avenue. Don bought the license, and Fern the rings. Richard and Katherine Lack stood up for them, and after the ceremony the newlyweds had dinner at the historic Lowell Inn in Stillwater. They honeymooned on Lake Superior, after a drive to Duluth in Don's rejuvenated Plymouth. Their honeymoon suite at the new Edgewater Motel on the waterfront cost them $14.50, according to Fern's record of expenses. The next morning the couple started up Minnesota 61—the North Shore Drive into Canada.

The moment that an artist takes notice
of what other people want and tries to supply the demand,
he ceases to be an artist and becomes a dull or an amusing craftsman,
an honest or a dishonest tradesman.

Oscar Wilde

Additions

FERN KOESTNER UNDERSTOOD "GETTING BY." At age 25, she already drew upon a deep reserve of hard-life experience. Growing up, she lived in a succession of homes along the Mississippi River, for a time on a small farm with a view of Lake Pepin. There, she and her seven younger siblings had responsibility for several cows, which they milked and led to pasture, plus pigs and chickens. Later the family rented a tiny house in the village of Bay City. The house was built on a hillside, just feet from the railroad tracks that ran between the highway and the river. Trains roaring through made the walls tremble. Smoke and cinders from the steam locomotives soiled the Monday laundry hanging on the clothesline. The house lacked indoor plumbing.

Now married, Fern looked not for luxury but for a few conveniences. Soon after their wedding, she helped Don with a home-improvement plan. Together, they designed an addition including separate kitchen, bath, studio, and bedroom—the combined square footage of which would more than double the cabin's original footprint.

Many of the planned upgrades involved engineering beyond Koestner's ability to contrive. He knew he could not drill a hole through hundreds of feet of limestone to tap into a sustainable water supply, but he had a skilled and reliable neighbor who could. He also needed someone with plumbing experience to install a system of pipes and drains below the frost line, and in the house a hot-water heater, bathtub, and sinks.

The estimated cost for all of this brought Koestner to another crossroads. So far he had managed to create his own shelter with minimum expense—never spending a dollar he did not have. Now, only by borrowing money could he and Fern hope to complete the planned projects before winter set in.

Borrowing money and buying on credit had become a common practice for most Americans in the postwar era, a new way of life. But Koestner used only cash. He seldom bought anything new *or* secondhand. Nor did he set money aside to cover himself for sickness and old age. Perhaps the specter of infirmity never took root in his mind because insurance agents and certified financial planners could not find his door. Instead, he maintained an optimism that "things will work out." And so far they had.

Because Don bought everything with cash, he lacked a credit history. As a single woman, Fern had established a credit rating, but she was a suspect borrower once she married "that artist living in a shack on the river." Don's association with Rex Jeremy, the river rat, didn't help his reputation with the bank. Despite some concerns, the Bank of Hastings approved a one-year construction loan for $1,000—with Jack Koestner as cosigner. (Jack saw his son's marriage as a move toward normalcy and was glad to be of help.) As collateral on the loan documents, the bank accepted Fern's car, valued at $300, and a used refrigerator Koestner bought for $10. The loan officer saw no value in Koestner's cabin and five acres of land—or in his nine-year-old Plymouth, despite its rebuilt engine and decent tires.

Don and Fern anguished over their decision to go into debt. To pay off the loan in the shortest possible time, the two immediately took full-time jobs in the city. Fern's perky voice and personality landed her a customer-service job with Northwestern Bell Telephone Company in St. Paul, but she quit after six months of listening to complaints all day long and returned to her old job at Chalet Studio in Red Wing. Her former boss was glad to have her back. Don became an instructor for a Minneapolis art school.

—⚹—

ART INSTRUCTION SCHOOLS (AIS), located in downtown Minneapolis, is remembered by some as the "Draw Me" school because of its widely distributed advertising on matchbook covers and in popular magazines. The ad invited people to copy a drawing and return it for a "no obligation" evaluation of their talent. A salesman followed up. Founded in 1914, the correspondence school had thousands of students across the United States and Canada, many seeking a creative outlet or second career. Students ranged from high-school kids often living in rural areas, to people long past retirement but still harboring dreams of self-expression. The prospect of becoming an artist—"learning in your own home and on your own schedule"—had enormous appeal.

The school's curriculum included specialized instruction in advertising art, fashion design, cartooning, painting, and illustra-

Gallery of Landscape Paintings

Evening Thunderheads, 1986

Baptism River, Afternoon, 1972

Sunrise Through the Birches, 1989

The Lone Farm, 1987

Early Morning Autumn, 1993

Baptism River, Early Spring, 1995

Summer Sunset, 1983

Beaver Dam, 1996

An April Evening, 1983

The Red Oak, 1994

Mountain Elderberry, 1987

Beaver River, Spring Runoff, 2002

Beaver, 1996

The Birchwood Morning, 1988

Winter Sunset, 1992

Northwoods, Autumn, 1998

tion. Illustrated study materials were covered by tuition. A teacher experienced in the student-subscriber's special-interest area provided instruction on basic lessons with a variety of form letters, sometimes dictating a letter to more advanced students. It was a thriving business.

A home-study art school seemed an unlikely setting for Koestner and for most of the talented painters, illustrators, and cartoonists who carried lunch pails to this workplace, punched a time clock, and evaluated student work for eight-hour stretches, five days a week. Koestner knew many of them. Fellow instructors in 1960 included his art-school friends Richard Lack, Chuck Gravem, and Cliff Moen—all now married and raising children. Working at AIS helped them pay their mortgages and clothe and feed their families. A dance with the devil, some said. But these were practical artists, trying to make a living with their knowledge instead of their art. Spending a good part of their days in cubicles instead of in their own studios was a compromise they were willing to make.

The school boasted one or two former instructors with broad success. One was Charles (Sparky) Schulz, a former student of Art Instruction Schools who taught there until launching his famous *Peanuts* comic strip. One of the *Peanuts* characters was inspired by fellow AIS instructor Charlie Brown.

Few of the instructors were happy in this commercial teaching environment, but fewer felt the agony of being away from their easels more than Koestner. Although he "hated his time there," he did his job conscientiously, often taking more time correcting and advising his home-study students than the management guidelines allowed. The pressure put on him to work faster sometimes kept him awake nights. He vowed he would work full time for no more than a year.

During the period that Fern worked for the phone company,

the Koestners commuted together to their jobs in the Twin Cities, Fern feeding Don hard-boiled eggs she had prepared the night before, so he could keep both hands on the wheel, his eyes grimly focused on the looming gray cityscape ahead. Cliff Moen did a cartoon of the commuting painter eating an egg, with Fern saying: "Oh, just think of it as a picnic, dear."

That summer, Koestner punched out the moment the time clock hit 4:30, picked up Fern in St. Paul, and rushed back to Nininger so he could get in several hours of carpentry. He devoted his weekends to the building project.

To prepare the addition site, Koestner excavated as much of the foundation and septic-tank area as he could with a spade and wheelbarrow. There was not much soil above the bedrock to remove. Then he hired a man known locally for his experience with dynamite. The explosives expert quickly completed the excavation, blasting holes deep enough to bury the septic tank and sewer tiles. The unorthodox contractor used a horse to help move large rocks and to dredge and refill the site. When he was done with the project, he left his horse to roam on Koestner's property for several months. When he neglected to send a bill for the blasting and filling, Koestner located his home in a trailer park near Hastings and gave the check to his wife.

A neighbor, Bud Crandall, drilled a 200-foot well and installed a submersible electric pump. Koestner shopped for fixtures. He eventually bought a used kitchen sink, bathtub, water heater, and most of the required plumbing supplies.

Koestner and his helpers laid the addition's foundation with cinder blocks, which he learned had better insulating quality than concrete and were superior to the wood foundation he had installed in 1952. He discovered that ground moisture quickly took its toll on wood because of the bluff area's high humidity.

Much of the above-ground framing for the addition was done

with drift lumber. But scouting the countryside nearby, Koestner made another find. Lying in tall weeds on a former farm site that had been cleared for the construction of an oil refinery were several barn beams—20 feet long, 8 inches square, and straight as a pin. Convinced they would rot if left there, he transported them to Nininger to use for floor supports and window headers on the addition.

While Koestner worked full time at the art school, his former boss, Pete Peterson of the cab company, did much of the cabin expansion. Peterson had suffered a run-in with the Internal Revenue Service for nonpayment of taxes and recently lost his business—cabs and all. With a young family to support, he needed work.

To pay Peterson, Koestner used some of the thousand-dollar bank loan, plus the better part of his $75 weekly earnings as an instructor. His former employer worked full time on the project for six weeks, building the addition's foundation and cinder-block walls, and doing plumbing and electrical work.

Koestner did most of the carpentry himself. On long summer evenings he did inside work, and on weekends his father helped him install roof rafters that he had cut and assembled on the floor but couldn't put up alone. Glen Raney, one of Koestner's former teachers at the Minneapolis School of Art, also came out to help. He contrived a way to lengthen the original cabin's rafters by attaching 2 x 4 extensions. Cousins Roy Ehlert and Art Koestner helped with roofing.

In another move toward comfort and convenience, Koestner replaced the woodstove with an efficient kerosene-burning Jungers heater given them by Carl Schaar, a farm neighbor. Koestner operated the heater with fuel stored in two 50-gallon oil drums he located outside the house. This stove allowed him to burn a low fire when they were gone and eliminated a lot of the woodcutting chores (he still used his fireplace). Both the kitchen stove and water heater ran on propane.

Next was bridge construction. Koestner's 10-year-old home-made bridge across a gully that separated the cabin from the main road collapsed while crossing it with a trailer-load of lumber. He constructed a new bridge, spanning the gully with telephone poles scavenged from the river. Neighbor Bill Hildt dragged the poles to the cabin from the landing at Walt's Cave with his tractor. Koestner supported the poles on pillars of concrete block and across them laid four-inch-thick creosoted planks, each eight feet long and bolted down. These came from a torn-down bridge that had once spanned the Mississippi near Newport. When the project was complete, Don and Fern held a ribbon-cutting ceremony. Invited guests included cousins Art Koestner and Roy and Arnie Ehlert, and their wives.

The Koestners paid off their construction loan in six months rather than a year, easing both their concerns about indebtedness. Nevertheless, Don continued working for Art Instruction Schools full time until the following June. Then he and fellow instructor Paul Van Demark, a commercial illustrator and close friend, worked out an arrangement for each working half-time at the school. Over the next nine years, with patience and resolve, Koestner worked his half-week down to zero days.

—⁂—

FERN BROUGHT A NUMBER OF ESSENTIAL QUALITIES to the couple's frugal life in Nininger. She wasn't an experienced cook—their first home-cooked meal consisted of hot dogs and beans. She had learned basic cooking skills in a high-school home-economic class, but that was years earlier, and she was out of practice—at least as to cooking from scratch. To stretch their food budget, she bought bulk supplies, "no mixes." She grocery-shopped with coupons and favored no particular store or label, often buying house or generic brands. She mixed butter with Canola Oil (unsaturated fat), fifty-fifty. Generous neighbors sometimes supplied the Koestners with fresh produce from their gardens.

As a wedding gift, the couple received a *Better Homes and Gardens* all-purpose domestic-living guide, and Fern assured herself: "If you can read, you can cook." As she plunged into roasting and baking, she got advice from more experienced friends and Don's mother, Frieda. (A telephone was part of the 1960 cabin overhaul.) In time, she learned to can fruits and vegetables.

There was an abundance of "nuts and berries" food foraging and dietary guides in the 1960s. These ranged from nutritionist Adelle Davis's *Let's Eat Right to Keep Fit* to wild-food gatherer Euell Gibbons's *Stalking the Wild Asparagus*. Davis, writing in the 1950s, cautioned against the consumption of artery-plugging foods: "As I see it, cholesterol deposition and its many related problems can be expected to get worse each year." Gibbons, in 1962, encouraged readers to explore nature's storehouse of edible food. "The idea of 'reaping where I did not sow' has fascinated me all my life," the forager wrote. Most such books were available in $1.50 paperback editions—and for 50 cents or less as used books. A voracious reader, Fern studied them all.

The cabin addition was mostly furnished and equipped with items found at Goodwill and Salvation Army stores, plus wedding gifts. Clothes, furniture, and other domestic paraphernalia often came to them as high-quality hand-me-downs from friends and relatives eager to clean out closets or redo rooms. Occasionally Fern bought a special item at a store's seasonal sale. The Koestners owned, bought or received little that was frivolous.

Early on, and periodically, there were health issues. The Koestners lacked medical insurance but made arrangements with local doctors to pay medical bills over time. Don began to experience lower back pain, perhaps caused by lifting. A doctor prescribed a series of stretching exercises that he faithfully followed from then on; occasional episodes of back pain continued but were less frequent. In 1961, Fern had a tubal pregnancy that was resolved with abdominal surgery. She was 26, healthy, and lucky. Following a successful recovery from her emergency operation—tubal pregnancies can be life-threatening if misdiagnosed—she again became pregnant. This time events proceeded normally.

Frederick John Koestner was born on January 20, 1963. Don added a bedroom for Frederick on the southeast corner of the house, adjoining the stone room. On May 1, 1964, Lorna Marie Koestner was born. Eventually, Lorna got her own bedroom when Don built a new studio on the north side of the original cabin, facing the river.

The Koestners' annual income through these years varied, but with both of them working it averaged between $5,000 and $6,000. They lived on less than $500 a month. Expenses included groceries, propane fuel and kerosene for the stoves, telephone and electricity, house and car insurance, gas for their two cars, medical bills, real estate taxes ($60 on the expanded cabin in 1961), and a few other essentials. Don did most of the car upkeep himself; when needed, Lee Lyon provided his expertise at a reasonable rate. A third, and sometimes half, of their income came from Fern's work retouching and coloring photos for several photo studios. This work she was able to do at home.

The Koestners lived well and contentedly—Don always more relaxed than Fern. Fern was fully engaged in their children's well-being. She met regularly with several other young mothers in the neighborhood. The young mothers' support group—five babies were born within six weeks of each other—met on Thursday mornings, drank coffee, and exchanged harrowing tales about fevers and rashes.

Koestner—39 when Fred was born and 40 at Lorna's birth—took fatherhood in stride.

"Quite lightly," Fern said.

"Having children is just one of those things that happen in life," Don said. Painting was always his anchor. Other parts of his life "kind of flowed around it."

—⁓—

DISCOVERY AND FULFILLMENT permeated almost everything Koestner did—whether painting, grinding pigments to make his own paint, house building, cutting wood—and for several years being a husband and father. In Fern, he had found someone who believed in his talent, and who supported him in every way. His life was in balance and fuller than it had ever been.

After the cabin renovations were complete, Koestner settled into a routine of painting—outdoors in good weather, mainly indoors during winter. Sometimes he used figures in his landscape paintings. Fern occasionally modeled, though reluctantly when it involved the outdoors. The scenic Mississippi, convenient to them at Nininger, presented Koestner many opportunities. But for his delicate, fair-skinned model, the river meant sun, wind, humidity, bug bites—and sometimes unexpected visitors.

One Sunday morning, Koestner used his homemade pontoon boat to tow Fern (seated in an old wooden rowboat) to a secluded spot he favored for painting. Once there, he set two anchors to hold her boat in place. Then he went downstream about 50 feet, anchored the pontoon, and set up his easel and canvas. It was a warm morning, and as Don quietly painted, Fern unzipped the back of her dress to cool off. At that very moment she heard a man's voice call out behind her: "How far to Hastings?" Two young canoeists had paddled downriver from St. Paul to attend church. Fern was startled. The paddlers were embarrassed, not knowing how much more of the artist's model they might have seen had they not called out.

The river could also test Koestner's dedication. On another morning, again with Fern's rowboat anchored offshore, a sudden gust upset his easel. Several expensive brushes went overboard, and Koestner could see them bobbing downstream in the current, their ferrules pointing to the river bottom. He quickly stripped to his shorts and jumped in to rescue them. Successful, he climbed back on the pontoon's deck and dripped dry while continuing to paint.

Throughout the 1960s, Koestner entered his work in competitive shows. These included the Minnesota State Fair and Ogunquit (Maine) Art Center annual shows—where he won awards for his painting. He also won a cash award from the American Artists Professional League at the New York Grand National Show. They weren't major prizes, but the recognition reinforced his belief that his work was improving. During this period he had several one-man shows, one at the College of St. Thomas (now a university) in St. Paul and another at the Maryhill Museum in Maryhill, Washington. While sales were not dramatic, his painting income began to rise above the $500 a year he had averaged in the 1950s. When his state fair winner sold for $400, the Ehlert and Koestner cousins expressed amazement that anyone would pay that much for a painting. Jack Koestner was impressed with the "national notice" his son received and by what complete strangers would pay for one of his paintings. It was proof that his son was good at what he did. Eventually, Jack bought a Don Koestner painting for $400 and hung it in his living room for visitors to admire.

Koestner was careful not to let painting sales or recognition become the measure of his success. He had seen that yardstick develop in some of the younger artists he knew, and it felt foreign to him.

"They do things more in the aspect of career," he said. "And to me, painting is just something I do. I never think of it as career work." Nevertheless, there was an unavoidable involvement with commerce in every artist's life.

Art galleries play a vital role in an artist's ability to reach an audience. Gallery owners not only provide wall space for an exhibit but also promote the event among likely art buyers and do some selling. At least there is reasonable expectation of that effort on the artist's part. Particular business approaches, as well as artistic sensibilities, varied. Koestner's first show, in 1958, was at an obscure St. Paul gallery called Alley 29. The owner priced paintings not on their quality, but strictly on size.

When Koestner began to sell his work, galleries typically took a third of the painting's sale price as a commission. Later, a 60/40 split became common, with the gallery taking 40 percent. Some wanted 60 percent. A few, like one gallery in Kansas City that sold a Koestner painting, attempted to take everything from the sale. When the gallery ignored Koestner's letters for payment, he sent a telegram. When that drew no response, he drove to Kansas City to confront the gallery owner, only to find that he had gone out of business; Koestner's telegram was taped to the door. After talking to the local Better Business Bureau about his experience, he located the owner at his home and finally got, in cash, the $50 he was owed. The owner was amazed that an artist would drive so far to retrieve his painting or get his money. The cunning dealer had a storage room full of paintings by artists who did not take the trouble. The thousand-mile round-trip, factoring in gas, motel, and several meals, cost Koestner nearly as much as he collected—not including his time. But the principle of nonpayment got his goat—an art merchant's dishonest act based on an assumption that artists are easy game—and he could not let it pass.

Koestner seldom sought out galleries. "I never liked the idea of a gallery breathing down my neck for the next painting," he said, "and I tried to avoid commissions for the same reason." Nevertheless, if a gallery offered to show his work, he was usually willing to assemble a dozen or so framed paintings from his expanding inventory.

Traditional painters such as Koestner were largely ignored by the art establishment of museums, galleries, art schools, and critics. The traditional group felt left out—worse yet, "dismissed"—by the mainstream powers that denied them notice. Koestner's irritation with them ran to a deeper level, to their persistent "tearing down of existing values and scoffing at the centuries-old endeavor of artists to create beauty." Always focused on his work, he moved on rather than dwell on a cultural climate over which he had no control. He found painting in nature infinitely challenging and satisfying—it was reward enough.

Occasionally, someone in the press did recognize Koestner's work. Following the opening of a one-man show in the late 1960s, veteran *Minneapolis Tribune* arts critic John K. Sherman wrote: "There's a vast pleasure in seeing the real world, that is the recognizable world, dealt with in terms of such truth of vision and affectionate precision as are found in the canvases of Don Koestner."

Don O'Grady, city editor of the *St. Paul Dispatch*, also supported Koestner's early work and bought several of his paintings over the years. In 1959, O'Grady assigned reporter Jim Carney to do a story on the artist. Carney, however, had difficulty arranging the interview because Koestner didn't have a phone. He then sent him a telegram, which went unnoticed on the artist's rural mailbox for a week. A call to Koestner's sister, Lorraine, living in Bloomington, was of little help since she had no way of reaching him either. Eventually the dogged reporter found the artist and wrote his story. "Simple, frugal and somewhat Bohemian," *Dispatch* writer Carney described Koestner. "His way of life has slipped out of fashion in today's chrome-plated world."

—⟞⟋⟍—

IN 1968, THE GOODHUE COUNTY HISTORICAL SOCIETY MUSEUM in Red Wing commissioned Koestner to paint a diorama depicting Red Wing as the Native American village it had been a hundred years earlier. The 10-by-20-foot painting was to serve as a background for an exhibition of artifacts in the museum's permanent collection. Conscientious about how to portray dress of the early period, Koestner examined the Seth Eastman paintings in the Minnesota Historical Society's collection. Eastman's 1840s depictions of frontier life along the Mississippi River south of St. Paul, painted while he was an army officer at Fort Snelling, gave Koestner the authenticity he sought. Koestner's realistic painting not only of the early landscape but its figures and objects was so realistically rendered that the diorama continues to draw comment today. Fern, dressed in mock native attire, modeled for a number of the poses he needed.

Empowered by the $2,000 commission, Koestner began looking for land on the north shore of Lake Superior, where Fern and he had honeymooned eight years earlier. They had returned to the area every summer, usually renting an inexpensive cottage for a week at Dean's Cabins near Castle Danger. Over the years, they became friends with the owners, Nellie and Dean Magnuson. Koestner felt increasingly drawn to the northern scenery and especially to the powerful waves and rocky cliffs. These landscapes were in stark contrast to the gently rolling wooded hills and farmland he knew so well. His intent was to build a cabin his family could use during school vacations. By this time he had reduced his time at Art Instruction Schools to one day a week, and soon he planned to resign. The family could then spend entire summers on the North Shore.

"To a more conventional couple with young children, quitting a salaried job and going off to build a cabin would have seemed irresponsible," Koestner said, "but Fern agreed to the decision. In our years of generally hand-to-mouth existence we adopted the phrase, 'Oh, something will turn up,' and it always did whenever money got troublingly low."

Adventurous campers, hikers, and canoeists had been visiting Minnesota's rugged northeastern region ever since President Theodore Roosevelt established the Superior National Forest in 1909. In the early days, access to this wilderness area was exclusively by foot, steamship and rail. A road for automobiles opened in 1925, the Lake Superior International Highway—or North Shore Drive. It continued from Minnesota into Canada.

In the 1960s, land prices rose on the North Shore. To find a place the Koestners could afford would require months of searching. Working with area realtors, Koestner looked at dozens of properties. Several he explored during the late summer and fall of 1968 were near Silver Bay, a town about 60 miles from Duluth. One parcel was priced at $3,500—more than he could afford. Several other lots, listed for $1,500, were too close to the taconite processing plant that flanked the shore.

Seeking a quiet spot that would allow him to view the world's largest lake—as measured by surface area, about the size of Maine—Koestner visited a herring fisherman's weather-beaten cottage. It was a wonderful spot near the shore. Alas, the price was $35,000.

One day he explored with a commercial-fisherman-turned-real-estate-agent a nearly two-acre lakefront parcel a few miles upshore from Silver Bay. It was late afternoon when he reached the spot. A chest-high thicket of thimbleberries, growing among birch, balsam fir, spruce, and pine trees, covered the property. A trail along one edge followed a mowed fence line to a cliff overlooking a small, sandy beach 35 feet below. Following the cliff's edge, Koestner saw below him a massive stone arch formed by the pounding waves, and beyond it a rocky island glowing fiery orange in the sparkling blue lake. The views of the lake and the blue-shaded arch stunned him. "This is it!" he said to himself. He didn't reveal his enthusiasm to the realtor, but he was sold on the place.

Eager to move on the opportunity, Koestner returned in mid-November with Fern and his parents. He needed Fern's consent, but he also wished to share his discovery with his father. Ever cautious, Jack Koestner objected to the trip because it was deer-hunting season and the former hunter was sure they'd get shot. Plus, he doubted they would find a place to stay overnight. But Don was determined to go, and he persuaded his father to come along. "Let's see what happens," he said.

Koestner's relationship with his dad had continued to improve since the births of Fred and Lorna. While Jack remained skeptical of his son's impractical vocation and rustic lifestyle, he now saw him living a fairly normal life. Both Jack and Frieda enjoyed their new grandchildren, often commenting on how well-behaved they were and how they entertained themselves in quiet play. Fern and Frieda also had a good relationship. Physically they were similar—both were small women, full of motion.

The Koestners found overnight lodging in nearby Beaver Bay, Don and Fern in a bunkhouse and Jack and Frieda in a primitive cottage with no running water. The lodge's outhouse was set on planks across a creek that flowed from the uplands to the lake. The next morning they walked through fresh snow onto the property together. "Fern was as happy as I," Don said.

Jack could see that his son had found another good piece of land. He was especially impressed with the trees. "Boy, you've got good birch lumber here," he said. "You can make some money on that." Don had no intention of cutting trees for lumber or cordwood; still, he understood Jack's opportunistic viewpoint, though he didn't share it. His father, he said, was "speaking for his generation."

This was the second time Koestner purchased land with money from commissioned work and the second time that some combination of persistence, instinct, and luck led him to "the perfect spot." The price, $2,500, was $500 more than he received for the Red Wing diorama, but he and Fern assured themselves that his prospects for selling paintings were solid enough to warrant a short-term loan. The Bank of Hastings obliged them again. They bought the property and during the winter drew up plans for a cabin-studio on the big lake.

The spring of 1969 brought flooding to the Mississippi River, and with the rising water came an abundance of bridge timbers, creosoted poles, railroad ties, and other usable building materials. "More Koestner luck," friends said. The artist salvaged two-thirds of the framing lumber he needed for the North Shore cabin, and stacked it to dry.

Having learned from a Hastings friend that board and batten would be a good and inexpensive way to enclose the proposed cabin, Koestner next contacted the owner of a small lumber mill 30 miles north of Silver Bay. Its owner, Bob Silver, agreed to mill and deliver enough cedar boards and 1-by-2-inch batten strips to cover a 12-by-16-foot cabin and a 3-by-4-foot outhouse.

Koestner's first project was building a road on the property and an outdoor toilet. To frame the outhouse, he cut and labeled 2 x 4s. On Memorial Day weekend, 1969, the Koestner family headed north in its 1957 Chevrolet with framing lumber tied to a roof rack, plus shovels and rakes for the road building. The family shoveled gravel for five days. Yards of it had been dumped in several large piles, the terrain too irregular for the truck to spread it. The gravel hauler, who lived a few miles north of Silver Bay, suggested that Koestner hire a bulldozer. When Koestner told him he couldn't afford that and would spread it by hand, the trucker lent him an extra shovel. Don and Fern spread it all with shovels and rakes. The kids—Frederick was six and Lorna five—helped out. To pack it down, Don drove his car back and forth like a roller. The labor-intensive method reminded him of the Chinese method of building runways during World War II, except that there the workers had numbered in the hundreds.

During June, Koestner hauled eight trailer loads of cabin-building materials to the site from Nininger. He had precut and marked most of it to speed construction. On one of many trips back and forth that month, Lorna awakened from a nap on the floor of the station wagon and asked, "Are we going to the cabin or coming home?"

Koestner spent the first week of July framing the small cabin with the help of a Hastings friend, Bill Benjamin, son of early Hastings contact Harry Benjamin. Bill Benjamin had a tent trailer in which the two could sleep. The new cabin was given a distinctive gambrel roof inspired by Midwestern barns. Koestner enjoyed this reference to rural America, but Benjamin, who had a sense of humor, said it reminded him of a Dairy Queen. Once the cabin was sided and the roof was on, Fern and the children came up for the remainder of the summer. Koestner's parents also spent a few days there. Jack helped his son install windows.

Cabin construction was complete in a record 30 days, and by the end of July Koestner was painting again. He explored the lake from vantage points up and down the shore and found panoramic views of the northland's forests from higher elevations a few miles inland.

Money and art are far apart.
Langston Hughes

Simple Living

DON KOESTNER'S PAINTING LIFE was split between Nininger and the North Shore. The spring before building the modest cabin-studio at Silver Bay in 1969, he cut his teaching ties with Art Instruction Schools so that the family could live all summer on Lake Superior.

Almost 20 years after completing art school, Don's painting sales still did not provide enough to live on. But Fern, in charge of the family budget, determined that they could live at Silver Bay for three months on $300.

Don had earned that amount the previous winter doing pastel children's portraits in the Hastings area. To get orders—$35 a portrait—Fern made phone calls and went door-to-door with a sample portrait of Lorna. Sometimes Don got the subject to pose for him. He preferred that but more often worked from a snapshot provided by the family. He continued doing these "grocery money" portraits from 1968 until he got back into part-time teaching in 1970.

The Koestner children—Fred was 7 and Lorna, 6, in the summer of 1970—took for granted their family's ability to spend summers on the North Shore. The kids had no sense of being "poor." The fact that their parents seldom if ever bought anything new, never threw anything useful away, did not borrow money, and "made do" all seemed normal. They also accepted that their parents were a constant presence, almost always home or nearby.

Both Fred and Lorna were bright, imaginative, and sensible. Since their father would not allow a television in their Nininger home, they found their entertainment in books from the town library, in board games and crafts, and in imaginative play. Their parents read in the evening, and once Fred and Lorna were old enough to read, so did they.

Summer days at the cramped cabin at Silver Bay were spent largely outdoors. Both Fred and Lorna made friends with kids who lived nearby. Together they created forts in the tall thimbleberry bushes, built tree houses, made dams across the streams that tumbled into the lake, and camped on the beach in their dad's war-surplus pup tent. The property's 490-foot shoreline and 35-to-45-foot cliffs included a sandy beach with good skipping stones scoured and washed by the waves. The stones felt good in the hand, each one smooth to the touch and distinct in color and shape. Fred was given a rock identification book and soon developed an eye for spotting agates in the river mouths along the shore as well as on local gravel roads.

To provide access to the beach their first weeks at Silver Bay,

Koestner tied a heavy rope to a firmly rooted cedar near the cliff's edge. Knotting the rope every foot or so to give him a better hand-hold, he then braced his feet against the wall and descended the near-vertical wall like a mountain climber. He took the kids one at a time down to the beach the same way, carrying each on his shoulders. Lorna's first trip down was "terrifying," she remembered, but once at the bottom she forgot her fright. Koestner soon built a 28-foot ladder that reached a ledge 10 feet from the beach. The ladder had only a slight incline, so he anchored it to the rock wall. He made the sides out of rough-sawn cedar supplied by sawmill operator Bob Silver, and the rungs from recycled river lumber that he soaked in creosote to prevent rot. Using lag screws, he attached the top of the ladder to a section of creosoted tele-phone pole that he buried in the soil. A 12-foot aluminum ladder allowed the final descent from ledge to beach. After that, Koest-ner sometimes painted on the beach, which offered him a differ-ent perspective of the shore and island. Fern and the children also used the ladder so they could picnic, wade, and skip stones. The deep lake's cold temperature discouraged swimming.

By age 10, Fred and his playmate, David Torgerson, became so adept at scrambling up the ladders hand-over-hand and foot-over-foot that they could reach the top without breathing hard. Don and Fern gave their kids freedom to explore but also imposed strict rules: one was to stay on paths on the bluff and not get close to its ever-eroding edge; another was to use the ladder to get up and down and not attempt to scale the cliff from the beach because loose rocks could cause a fall. One day Fern happened along the path just as Lorna reached the top of a near-vertical cliff. Fern was so upset that she cried, scolding Lorna between sobs, "If I lost you, what would I do?" Lorna never did it again.

Summer activities at Silver Bay included picking berries, espe-cially wild raspberries growing along the roads. Fern and the kids laid them in pans to dry in the sun—a process that took only a day or two—then stored the hard, shriveled berries in jars. During the winter Fern reconstituted them with water. In late summer, they picked blueberries that grew among the rocks on Palisade Head, a towering bluff 10 miles from Silver Bay. Sometimes the berries were slow to ripen and the Koestners missed the September harvest. Summers often included a road trip east to visit art museums, and stops along the way to see relatives and friends.

Although Lorna shared her dad's closeness with nature, her mother was the one who introduced her to plants and flowers. Car trips along the North Shore were slowed by frequent stops so Fern and Lorna could identify wildflowers growing beside the roads—wild columbine, lupine, fireweed, blazing star, oxeye daisy. "Every flower was a daisy or pansy to dad," Lorna said.

Fern also identified birds and animal tracks and kept journals of what she observed. While Don tirelessly looked out upon sun-yellowed fields and green, wooded hills, Fern examined nature's details with a naturalist's eye. She preferred reading to physical activities, practiced arts and crafts, sewed and embroidered. She occasionally did cross-stitch designs and decorative note cards for a local souvenir shop.

Neither Don nor Fern were competitive or athletic, but both were tough in spirit and long on resolve. The examples they presented to their children were determination, resilience, and patience. Small for his age, Fred didn't enjoy rough play; a neighbor boy at Nininger beat him up one day. Once word spread that he was easy prey, other boys joined in the romp. They could make life miserable for him, so he kept his distance.

Lorna, 17 months younger, also had a gentle disposition. In the absence of playmates, the two siblings imagined friends in a world of their own making. At home in Nininger, living on a bluff that overlooked a 2,500-mile-long river, they invented a world they called "the Universe." When a neighbor moved away, Lorna and Fred adopted their son's names and called themselves Renny and Doc—Rulers of the Universe. Accompanying Renny and Doc on their adventures through the woods and fields near home were a stuffed cat and stuffed bear. Fred and Lorna also played in neighboring cornfields, a mysterious and exciting hide-and-seek environment when the cornstalks towered three feet above them. They played some on the bluff, but as youngsters they weren't allowed to go down to the river alone.

Don always had a boat for use on the river, and he and Fern sometimes took the kids for a ride. Their first boat was a homemade pontoon, then an aluminum johnboat with a flat bottom and square ends designed for shallow waterways. In the early 1970s, Don bought a kit for building a "Folboat," a small craft resembling a kayak he saw advertised in *National Geographic*. He constructed the frame on his studio floor, covering the hull with a durable Naugahyde fabric. The family used the boat to explore backwaters of the Mississippi; after building the Silver Bay cabin they used it on Lake Superior and on smaller lakes.

The Koestners' lifestyle required an unwavering dedication to economy and conservation practices. Specifically: buy only what you need; if possible, buy used goods; fix and mend things when they wear out; try to make what you need from scratch.

Lorna recalled her mother's experiment with making bread from scratch, buying wheat in bulk from the grain elevator in Hastings and grinding it by hand to produce a coarse flour.

"Fred and I didn't like this period in our dietary history," Lorna said. "First of all, we were conscripted to grind the kernels, a task both difficult and boring, the finished product dense and crumbly. We called it 'brick bread.'"

Fern saved for reuse almost every manufactured product passing through her hands. Her "siege mentality" storage closets in

Nininger were packed with empty toilet-paper rolls and thread spools (for Christmas tree ornaments); bottles and jars of various sizes; a bag of used plastic bags; bags of buttons and zippers from old clothes; scraps of construction paper; empty egg cartons and stacks of used wax paper; reusable writing paper, envelopes and bags; buttons, ribbons, and bows; spools of used wire and string and other fasteners. Don saved used nails and screws.

An artist planning to help Don clean 35mm transparencies of his paintings asked whether she should bring along some cotton for wiping the film. "Don't bother," Don said. "I have a whole jar of cotton balls that Fern has saved from aspirin bottles."

Fern's penny-pinching was legendary among friends. A St. Paul art-gallery owner once heard her scold a parking meter because the required quarter was excessive for the dime's worth of time she needed to complete her business.

"My, you *are* a tightwad, aren't you?" the gallery owner said.

In the 1960s and 1970s, before community landfills were outlawed, the Koestners made routine visits to town dumps near Nininger and Silver Bay. These were heaped with many reusable items: kid's bikes, car wheels, shovels and rakes with broken handles, outdated home appliances in working condition, cooking utensils, furniture, bed frames, games, toys, books. Fred and Lorna viewed the visits as treasure hunts. There was something satisfying about taking castoffs and putting them to good use, and they often came home from the dump with more than they had hauled there. Don once found an army winter dress uniform in his size and in perfect condition. He used the durable wool trousers when painting in the cold outdoors.

Water conservation had been Koestner's practice from his bachelor days, when he drew all his cooking and wash water from the Mississippi River. (In the 1950s, the river water below St. Paul was still fairly clean.) Even after he got his well to work and installed a hand pump, he continued to conserve water.

When Koestner built the cabin at Silver Bay in 1969, he devised a way to draw his water supply from Lake Superior. He was reassured of the water's safety by a Twin Cities physician who pumped drinking water for his own lakeshore cabin from a pipe extending to the rocky beach. The doctor had the water tested for *ecoli* bacteria and told Koestner it was drinkable.

To access the lake water from his bluff 35 feet above the shore, Koestner constructed a heavy-duty A-frame with a 16-foot-long 2 x 6 at its apex—nearly half the beam extending beyond the cliff. Beneath it, he attached an 8-foot-long 2 x 2 with a barn-door pulley on one end. This apparatus served as a trolley along which Koestner could move a water pail horizontally along the beam, lower it into the lake, then raise the filled pail on a rope he had wound around a car-wheel rim fitted with a left-handed crank. Koestner filled two pails a day—occasionally a third—and carried them up the slope to the house, a distance of 220 feet. "It's surprising how little water you have to use when you watch your use of it," he said. All the construction material came from the Mississippi, the pulley from a barn razed near Hastings.

Use of the lake's water for drinking came into question in June 1973 when the Environmental Protection Agency issued a warning about high concentrations of asbestos fiber found in the water supply of Duluth and several communities on the Minnesota shore of Lake Superior. The source was Reserve Mining Company's discharge of taconite-processing wastes into the lake at its Silver Bay plant. During the seven-year legal battle that waged until dumping ceased in 1980, North Shore residents sought other sources for drinking water. Many bought bottled water, but the Koestners filled jugs at Duluth's water-filtration plant, a convenient source on the their way to the cabin or on routine visits to the city. Another free source of drinking water was an artesian well near the village of Finland, several miles inland.

A few years after building the cabin at Silver Bay, an artist friend who had property on the shore told Don about another water source. In most places along the North Shore, the soil was only a foot or so above the rock that formed the bluffs; constant summer runoff from the hills above them formed underground streams. One day, Fred told his dad about a swampy spot he discovered while digging on the slope above the house. Don doubted the water would be drinkable, though it would be somewhat filtered through the thin layer of soil. That winter, after cracking through an ice layer, he found clear water running beneath the ice. Realizing they had tapped into a spring, the Koestners thereafter drank that water during winter visits to the cabin.

The following spring Don devised a way to channel the surface water supply into the house. Using string and a carpenter's level, he marked a spot on the hill a foot or two above the level of the cabin's kitchen sink, then dug down far enough to install a catch basin—a box with a lid built of "drift plywood." Holes drilled into the uphill side of the box admitted water from the underground flow. Don then attached a garden hose to the cabin side of the box to direct the groundwater downhill and into the kitchen sink. The family could turn the water supply on and off at the faucet. It was a primitive system by 1970s plumbing standards, but it worked.

Inspired by the potential of this new water source, Koestner next experimented with a solar shower—a phone-booth-sized structure with a plate-glass roof built near the cabin. When it became clear that the trees around the shower prevented the sun from warming the ice-cold water supply coiled on top of the stall, he converted the booth to a stand-up bath. On crossbars at the top of the shower stall he mounted a washtub from his bachelor days in Nininger. At the bottom of the tub he installed a short hose with an on-off switch and beneath that, a showerhead made from the end of a sprinkling can. Into the groundwater hose leading to the kitchen sink, he spliced another hose that branched to the top of the shower stall. An on-off switch allowed him to feed five or six inches of water into the tub for the sun to warm. At shower time, he climbed a ladder to add a teakettle full of hot water.

With limited living and storage space—both at Nininger and Silver Bay—the Koestners were careful about what they accumulated. When Jack and Frieda Koestner died within eight days of each other in 1978, Don and his sister, Lorraine, each stood to inherit half a household of goods and furnishings acquired during their parents' married life. Don and Fern took only a few pots and pans, Frieda's rocking chair, and a box of Frieda's clothes—most of which fit Fern perfectly. They used some of the money inherited from the estate to finance a trip to Oklahoma and Texas with paintings Don hoped to exhibit in Southwest galleries. They enjoyed the two-week trip, but a year later Don had to retrieve the paintings because none had sold.

When Don Koestner's favorite relative, Uncle Frank, died during that period, Frank's daughter, Margaret, put much of her dad's belongings on the road for neighbors to pick through. Koestner took only Frank's scythe, so he could more efficiently cut the tall grass and weeds growing near the Silver Bay cabin and along the footpaths there. He still uses it.

Fern's talent, spunk, and resourcefulness helped to make the couple's frugal life both workable and harmonious. To free her husband to concentrate on his art, she managed the household; kept a budget and paid bills; looked after the children's needs; made social calls and wrote letters; baked, canned, cooked, and cleaned; and held a part-time job—all to keep their day-to-day life moving smoothly and inexpensively. She performed these duties with a cheerfulness that masked occasional bad days. She had early signs of a serious illness but didn't reveal it to many. "I put on a good face," she said.

Over the years, the Koestners gained a reputation for living well on little money. They were an inspiration to many young artists who visited and asked how the Koestners managed to live as well as they did. Frequent inquiries prompted Fern to write a plain-speaking essay in 1974; in it she offered this advice:

> After 14 years of living with an artist, I think I can say I'm an authority on the struggles of an artist to maintain his integrity without compromising himself . . . The secret to this kind of success is easy to explain but harder to follow. Rule number one: don't get in debt. If you must borrow or buy on time, let it be for as short a time as possible. Try to work full time to pay for it and then go back to a part-time job. The underlying philosophy is to take pride in owing no one anything and owning everything you have. Rule number two: Don't get married too early, before you've found out what you really want to do or before you are settled in a career.

Fern summarized her husband's dedication:

> [Don is] an artist who drove cab for two days a week earning enough to keep him for the rest of the week in a Walden-type setting, painting as he pleased. He drove 15-year-old cars, his standard of living was below the poverty level, but he didn't starve and he could tell the Establishment to [take a hike]. He was true to his dream, and that was back in 1951. Today [1974], he maintains himself in the same style, accompanied by a wife and two kids, only now he works [teaching] just one day a week, nine months a year. They live in a comfortable three-bedroom home during those nine months and in the summer in a lake cabin, [where] the artist works on his projects full time. They've discovered that too many "things" makes one unhappy—not happy.

—ɯ—

DON KOESTNER, 52 YEARS OLD IN THE SUMMER of 1976, had lived in Nininger for 25 years, 16 of them with Fern. Their children, Fred and Lorna, were 13 and 12. Between teaching income, painting sales, and Fern's work coloring black-and-white photographs, the family was able to meet basic needs. Unexpected expenses were met in various ways, sometimes by bartering for services. When Fred and Lorna needed braces for their teeth, a Rochester orthodontist provided braces in exchange for two paintings.

Throughout their preschool and grade school years, Fred and Lorna took for granted their dad's workaday life: painting in the studio or at some site on the river or in the woods. Unlike many kids, they knew precisely what their father did all day, and they did not view him as different from other dads. As a little girl, Lorna quietly watched how he developed images in his painting, first doing a pencil drawing on the canvas, then, with his brush, putting down blues and reds and yellows. She loved the reds and was disappointed when she did not see them in the finished painting. She thought the selection of colors and gradual buildup of paint on the canvas "an odd and amazing thing." Observing her dad draw pastel portraits, she came to understand his skill and patience. Far less patient, she found pastel drawing "annoyingly difficult."

Not until Fred and Lorna entered the social pressure cooker of junior high—one emphasizing an orthodox lifestyle and fashion standard—did they begin to realize the unusual nature of their dad's vocation. More-conventional fathers left home early in the morning and didn't return until evening. That their father was an artist who worked at home was for them a point of pride, even as it was peculiar to their schoolmates. That they had fewer things than most children also crept into their consciousness. In sixth grade, Lorna once asked her mother what she could donate to a school food-bank program. Fern said, "We're one of the families that should be *getting* food from the food bank, not donating to it" and explained their economic situation.

Fred and Lorna attended a large public high school in Hastings, three miles south of Nininger. They were eager to learn, had good study habits, and always completed their assignments. Both excelled in their studies; both were always on the "A" honor roll. Though quiet, they stood out from the crowd as odd and out of touch. They lacked the popular knowledge of TV shows, movies, and teen magazines; they wore good, but not "brand" clothes. Most of what Fred and Lorna wore came from relatives and friends cleaning closets of what their kids had outgrown or found out of fashion.

A school bus picked up Fred and Lorna every morning—they were among the last students on the route—and brought them home in the afternoon. Lorna managed fairly well on the bus rides, but Fred, who was small for his age, wore glasses, and always climbed on board with an armload of books, fell victim to taunts and scuffles and never found a seat. He hated the tortuous bus ride and eventually rode his bicycle to school, even in winter.

Physically Fred, except for his fair complexion, resembled his dad. Like his father in adolescence, Fred withdrew from social activities and participation in sports. He also had his dad's ability to focus his attention, and at home he built ship and airplane models. Although he showed a talent for drawing, his father did not push him to become an artist. Koestner believed that those born to the calling needed little encouragement, that the test of their calling was their persistence. Recalling his childhood interest in art, Fred said he "didn't have the inner drive to do what dad was doing." He nevertheless enjoyed observing the painting process from beginning to end, and sometimes helped his dad with picture framing. He liked being on the river, salvaging drift lumber with his dad. As Fred grew older he escaped into books, reading science fiction to the point of ignoring household chores. "It became an issue," Fred recalled of his reluctance to help around the house.

Lorna, with her paternal grandmother's black hair and brown eyes, remembers herself as "good at academics, excruciatingly shy, and pretty much a loner." The fifth through tenth grades were the worst time for her because she never felt accepted. She attributed that to a combination of her disposition and manner of dress. Most classmates saw her, she said with resignation, "as a mass of gray matter." With little social life, she pushed herself to engage in school activities. She played trumpet and baritone in the marching band and found fun in making music with others. She also joined the art club and Homemakers of America, then the Future Farmers of America, where she discovered an affinity for plants and flowers.

In their last years of high school, both Fred and Lorna were welcomed into a "born again" youth church group. There they found a social acceptance they had seldom experienced among fellow students. Their father frowned upon their new religious affiliation—nature was his church and it provided him all the inspiration and communion he needed—but his children clung to their convictions as stubbornly as he held to his.

Craftsmanship must again be made the solid foundation of art.
Max Doerner

Studio Craft

DON KOESTNER'S TIDY STUDIO IN NININGER measured 12-by-20-feet. This 1964 addition to his house had two north-facing windows admitting reliable north light through the changing seasons. Here he worked at a homemade easel considerably larger and sturdier than the portable one he used in the field. A circle of clear space in front of the studio easel allowed him to stand 18 to 24 inches from the canvas when he painted, with room to step back to view his work. There was ample space for a model to pose on a chair or swivel-seat stool some distance from the easel and to set up still-life objects on a table. A large vertical mirror, leaning against the wall when not in use, provided a reverse image of his canvas. This helped him to correct any visual bias as well as to see whether his dark and light tones provided adequate separation of key shapes in the composition. In the field, he used a small mirror for this purpose.

Collected on a small, adjustable table that he could elevate to a comfortable standing height—a former hospital table onto which he had mounted a draftsman's board—were paint tubes, brushes, palette knives, paint rags, and several cups and jars. Because his Nininger home had no basement for a workshop, the southeast wall of the studio included a workbench made from drift lumber. On one end of the bench was a heavy-duty vise. Attached to the other was a miter vise for clamping and cutting frame molding. (Fern, Lorna, and Fred helped Don in the finishing process, a craft in itself. To "age" the framing material for a traditional painting, they gilded the frames, then applied a gesso coat of glue, chalk, and a color pigment compatible with the painting.) A collection of various tools occupied a shelf below. Don normally had three or four paintings in progress. These canvases were leaned against the walls. Finished paintings were stored in a bedroom closet.

The door to the studio was always open, and the smell of oil paint and turpentine filled the home. From the time Fred and Lorna were old enough to be underfoot, they had learned that their dad's studio was off-limits. But Koestner enjoyed the sound of the children playing on the floor in the next room. Sometimes he invited them into the studio after supper to demonstrate how he ground paint, a process both found fascinating. Scraping up the remnants of oil paste with his palette knife, Don might magically form the shape of a school bus or clown. The children accepted as normal the smell of oil paint and the silence of a soft brush creating dabs of sunshine on a taut white canvas.

Koestner bought unprimed linen canvas in bulk and applied

his own base "ground" to the material. From experience, he learned that commercially prepared canvas had too much oil in the fabric, a condition allowing the vendor to roll the canvas for shipment without cracking it. The oil, however, made the canvas shiny and nonabsorbent. Wishing his paints to adhere strongly to the canvas, he began using a semiabsorbent ground of his own making. His recipe for the ground (a mixture of one-third rabbit-skin glue liquid, one-third titanium white pigment, and one-third chalk, to which he added boiled linseed oil) came from his revered manual on painting techniques and materials by Max Doerner. *The Materials of the Artist and Their Use in Painting with Notes on the Techniques of the Old Masters* was a compilation of Doerner's lectures over a 25-year period at the Academy of Fine Arts at Munich. In his preface to the American edition of the book, published in 1934, the German art professor observed: "When one considers how thoroughly Dürer, Leonardo, Rubens, Reynolds, and other masters studied their materials, one is tempted to smile at the fears of [the] many painters of today who believe that their personalities would suffer if they should concern themselves too closely with the craftsmanship of their art."

Following Doerner's traditional formula, Koestner also ground his own paint. He bought pigments from various sources in New York (such as Kremer Pigments). Grinding dry pigments to produce oil paint is a tedious practice, one that Koestner has continued to follow for more than half a century. He reserves the task for evenings and rainy days but out of it obtains colors of greater intensity than even the best commercial paints. It is important for him to know what he has in the paint tube and on his canvas, and he feels the standards for commercial paints are not reliable. "The manufacturers slant their product to amateur painters," he said. "Some cheap brands can contain as much as 30 percent nonpigment fillers such as chalk."

Oil paint has been the medium of choice for master painters going back centuries because paint made of pigment suspended in oil allows light to penetrate its many layers. This luminosity helps to create realistic effects.

To produce a five-ounce tube of oil paint, Koestner works at a table given him in the early 1950s by Hastings friend Roger Tonsager. (Tonsager built the table, a miniature version of a Scandinavian carpenter's bench, for his son as a Christmas gift. When the boy took no interest in it, Roger gave the bench to Koestner for a paint-grinding table.) Koestner fitted the top of the bench with a large piece of plate glass, the surface of which he roughened slightly by rubbing Carborundum and a little water with his paint muller. Koestner described his process:

> Preceding my use of the grinding table I stiffly mix the particular pigment with oil in a mortar and pestle. Different pigments require differing amounts of oil, the average being about one ounce of oil to one cup of pigment. With a spoon or palette knife, I put about a tablespoon of the stiff mixture on the grinding glass and spread it with the muller until a creamlike consistency results. That product is picked up with a palette knife and placed at a corner of the glass, and the procedure is repeated until all the paint is ground.
>
> In my early years of paint grinding I could reliably figure it took me one hour to fill a studio tube (37ml) with finished paint. To grind enough to fill a one-pound tube of white lead took me three hours. This held true until about the 1980s. After that time and to the present I can work three hours to fill a studio tube and no longer grind a full tube of white but grind only one cup of white lead and mix that with enough Old Holland white to fill my one-pound tube. Old Holland produces the best commercial paint I am aware of, but its lead white is too stiff to mix easily with my other colors. This change is due to the fact that I can no longer find a source of cold pressed linseed oil (the

preferred grinding oil for three or four centuries).

A year ago, I read some notes I'd made from a book on Frederic Remington given me by my son, Fred. There, I found that Remington mixed zinc white with his white lead. Experimenting, I ground a cup of zinc, and for reasons I don't understand, it combined better with the Old Holland white.

Koestner views the mastery of traditional painting techniques as an unending process—lifelong because there seems no limit to the learning, trials, and practice involved. To this self-taught artist, traditional painting is not "the mere copying of nature" but a challenging endeavor that tests one's knowledge, technical ability, visual acuity, and emotional and spiritual depth.

Underneath it all lie tried and tested studio techniques. According to Max Doerner: "Only a complete mastery of the materials will give that firm foundation on which the artist may develop an individual style and which at the same time will insure the durability and permanency of his creations."

Doerner stressed the importance of traditional training: "It is no more possible to learn to paint from books than to learn to swim on a sofa."

For an artist, half of learning to paint is learning to see. In a traditionally schooled painter's lexicon, seeing involves training the eye to see light and shadow on a figure or object, also to distinguish direct light from reflected light, and to perceive subtleties of color, form, and texture. Most of us tend to see mental images—a stored impression of reality, rather than what is truly before our eyes. Seeing is vital to achieving accuracy in drawing and painting.

Traditionally schooled painters also understand the visual bias that most of us have—often without knowing it—to slant things left or right. Our brain may tell us something is perfectly horizontal or vertical, when in fact it is not. Painters from as early as the sixteenth and seventeenth centuries have recognized this bias and used optics as a drawing aid. A double-convex lens and a small mirror set in a black box (camera obscura) projecting a reversed image helped painters see their compositions with a fresh eye. Vermeer, among others, is thought to have used the device.

Other painters accomplished the same accuracy check by viewing their works-in-progress in a black mirror. For years, Koestner has used a 5½-by-7-inch piece of plate glass painted black on the back. This lowers the value (degree of darkness) of objects reflected. When a painting and a subject being painted are reflected in the mirror simultaneously any discrepancy is easily spotted.

"Once," he said, "I had a bright green patch of grass in the sunlight appear higher in key than the sky. But my black mirror told me the sky was lighter."

A simple corrective device that Koestner uses to check the vertical orientation of objects in a drawing is an ordinary plumb bob. The method is especially helpful in painting outdoors. If the edge of the canvas is plumb, he can more accurately gauge the slant of a tree trunk or slope of a hill. He uses a carpenter's level to check horizontal relationships.

—ⱳ—

ALTHOUGH KOESTNER DID NOT SEEK opportunities to teach what he had learned largely through years of observation and practice, his experience and temperament made him an effective teacher. He said both student and teacher benefit. "The teacher has to be the objective eye for his students and that process hones one's own eye." Teaching also gave Koestner a sense of his own growth as a painter, and he found it gratifying to pass that experience along.

In the fall of 1970 Koestner received an unexpected request to teach a class at the Minnesota Museum Art School in St. Paul. The call came the night before the school's first morning class was to begin. He felt somewhat insecure about accepting the position because his teaching experience was limited to amateur groups. "I slept little that night but needn't have worried," he said. He found the school run haphazardly and his students much like those he had previously taught. After the first year of instructing a half-day drawing class, he taught a morning portrait-and-figure class, and an afternoon still-life class for four years.

For traditional painters such as Koestner, there is a mission in teaching the craft aspect of painting. He could help students not only to see, but also to develop drawing and compositional skills no longer taught in art schools and university art classes. Some of Koestner's beginning students were recently out of high school, others just out of college or working. Most who enrolled were eager to master art fundamentals—even if it took years.

Koestner said the Minnesota Museum Art School's administration, was "oddly inconsistent." Despite sponsoring his traditional drawing and painting classes for five years, the director refused to include Koestner's work in the museum's largely avant-garde exhibits. Koestner went to him several times to express interest in a show of his own, and was finally told, "I don't want to encourage your kind of art." At the end of the school year in 1975, the museum abruptly closed the school. Koestner, initially shocked by what amounted to a firing, was angry. For years, the school had displayed in a locked glass case a Koestner portrait of a child. He decided he wanted it back—immediately. When stalled by the director's secretary, Koestner fumed.

"The director's busy right now and can't see anyone," the secretary said.

"He'll see me," Koestner said and brushed past her into his office.

The shocked director immediately unlocked the display case and returned the portrait.

By coincidence, that same year Richard Lack relocated the studio-school he had started in Minneapolis in 1969. The school's curriculum and practices followed the rigorous apprenticeship model according to which Lack had trained for four years in Boston. Lack invited Koestner to teach an avocational afternoon class to help Lack pay the rent on his larger space. Koestner's former St. Paul students were delighted to hear their classes would continue in Minneapolis. Koestner taught there once a week for 10 years and supervised a class of Lack's full-time students during the last two.

The friendship of the two men went back to their student days at the Minneapolis School of Art in 1946. Because Lack was four years younger than he, Koestner had been impressed by his fellow student's "exceptional drawing skills." Lack also knew more than their teachers about the history of art, Koestner said, and about the aesthetics of painting, its form and beauty. Frustrated with MSA, Lack left after two-and-a-half years to look for training opportunities in New York. He wound up in Boston as a student of R. H. Ives Gammell, an accomplished painter whose own training linked him directly with master painters of the nineteenth century and earlier. Gammell had learned his craft in the studio-school of Boston impressionist painter William Paxton. Paxton had studied in Paris at the École des Beaux-Arts with Jean-Léon Gérôme, and so on back in an unbroken line of traditionally schooled painters to Jacques-Louis David.

Gammell's training in Boston may have resembled that of the first director of the Minneapolis School of Fine Arts, Douglas Volk, who studied under Gérôme for four years in the 1870s.

The study of human anatomy was central to academic training in art. Many American art schools in the 1880s provided "artistic anatomy" lectures by a local physician. American realist painter Thomas Eakins, another Gérôme student in Paris, had a passion for anatomy and went so far as to have his students at the Pennsylvania Academy dissect cadavers. He personally spent two years studying anatomy by dissection at the Jefferson Medical College in Philadelphia "to increase his knowledge of how beautiful objects are put together ... so that he might imitate them."

In 1946, Boston's R. H. Ives Gammell published a book on the demise of craft-based traditional painting. Titled *The Twilight of Painting*, he described in his book how art schools had abandoned the disciplines of traditional training. Lack and Koestner knew that only too well from their experiences at MSA. Gammell's training program was completely opposed to modernist trends, movements, and teaching methods. He recruited his students carefully, testing not only their raw abilities but also their desire and work ethic to learn through a rigorous system of studio practice and criticism. He wanted to know what a potential student read and thought about—what informed his consciousness. He didn't want slackers and whiners or shallow, half-hearted students taking up his time.

Lack served a four-year apprenticeship with Gammell and in his studio-school learned painting skills from the bottom up, doing rigorous drawing and painting studies, and eventually participating in the production of large canvases and murals under Gammell's critical and demanding eye. Gradually Lack mastered his craft.

When Lack returned to Minneapolis in 1957, the two art-school friends got reacquainted. Lack had recently married and settled in a partially completed new home in Glen Lake, a western Twin Cities suburb. Encouraged by the example of Koestner's self-built cabin at Nininger, Lack decided to build his own studio addition, and Koestner lent a hand.

Before the addition was complete, Lack sometimes painted in Koestner's studio. In one painting exercise they did together, each painted a portrait of the other. Here, Lack demonstrated a technique learned from Gammell: the "sight-size" method of drawing: The artist sets his canvas next to the subject—usually figure or still life—and views both of them together from a distance of 9 feet or so (depending on canvas size) to check the drawing's accuracy.

A few years later, Koestner and Lack worked together at Art Instruction Schools, where Lack was heralded as the national correspondence school's "Dean of Painters." He remained with the school until 1969, when he left to start his own school for the training of traditional painters—Atelier Lack.

In the 1970s, the studio-school training system caught on, and several of Lack's students went on to start their own. To reflect the group of painter's traditional roots, they called themselves "classical realists," a term Lack coined as the network expanded and began to publish a quarterly magazine.

Although Koestner associated with the classical realist group and felt bound by their common interest in traditional painting, he considered himself independent in terms of style—part realist, part impressionist—and more interested in landscape than studio painting. For the most part he had learned his landscape painting craft through personal study and by following his own course.

Art history books are filled with "ists" and "isms" to help classify painting styles from one historical period to the next, but Koestner saw more similarities than differences in the work of traditionally trained painters. "There's a kind of overlapping, " he said. "All good painters paint alike. Millet (realist) is akin to the impressionists in some of his work. You'll find examples of Sargent that could be taken for Degas, and Degas paintings that could be taken for Velazquez."

While painting outdoors is essential to a landscape painter, Koestner said successful picture making, particularly the design of compositions, is better handled in the studio. This environment allows more time than does outdoor painting for planning and properly blocking in a work. In his studio Koestner recreated the fast-changing light effects that were recorded in his oil sketches, thumbnail sketches, and memory. "In working out of doors," he said, "the tendency is to become overly influenced by the subject. Degas referred to it as 'losing consciousness in front of nature.'"

In an essay on studio painting published in 1985 in the book *Realism in Revolution*, Koestner described the experience:

> Design is often less considered, and unity more difficult to achieve, in a picture composed on the spot. It is difficult . . . to correct faulty underlying design (that combination of line and massing of dark and light shapes that adds up to a pleasing visual impression) out of doors. The problem of creating unity (that state in which a picture has a definite focus on a center of interest, and subordinate shapes, objects or colors retain their relative positions) can sometimes be better achieved by studio manipulation of color or value. For this reason, artists have often composed and executed landscapes in the studio.
>
> Studio painting is absolutely necessary to depict the poignant, fleeting effects of nature that do not repeat themselves. Here, one generally does not have even the luxury of a color sketch from which to work. A sunset, rainbow, or particular cloud effect can disappear in less time than it takes to set up easel and palette. I particularly like to paint such moods of nature and normally begin with a quick pencil sketch of shapes, along with some written notes on color.
>
> This is the most common method I have come to rely upon for capturing such phenomena. The method is not my invention. Sketchbooks of Turner, Moran, and many others contain annotated drawings. At times I will make a color sketch as soon

as possible afterwards, while my memory is fresh. Memory plays a large part in the production of any landscape done in the studio.

Although Monet sometimes claimed that he had no studio, that his studio was "the whole outdoors," his paintings reveal (and photographs confirm) that he worked over his paintings extensively in the studio. Koestner's studio landscapes are often a composite of observed elements. A beautiful cloud effect might be the motivation for a painting. But after that was noted, he would search for landscape components that were an appropriate setting for that sky. Later, in the studio, he would look through accumulated sketches to find other useful elements.

Koestner summarized the process in an essay on painting: "The experience of years of work and the consequent accumulation of knowledge is essential in producing a convincing finished picture of a fleeting effect. Such painting is not the province of the novice landscape artist, since it requires a combination of notes, memory, general knowledge, and invention."

Edgar Degas put it simply: "Painting is easy when you don't know how, but very difficult when you do."

One is born an artist. This craft is acquired through study,
observation, and practice; it can improve by ceaseless work.
But the instinct for art is innate. First, one has to love nature with all one's
heart and soul, and be able to study and admire it for hours on end.
William-Adolphe Bouguereau

Wild Delight

DON KOESTNER HAD RICH SOURCES of inspiration and subject
matter, and he painted outdoors in all seasons. To locate painting
opportunities, he traveled country roads, watching for pleasing
combinations of shapes: interesting buildings and trees, striking
light and dark contrasts, unusual light effects. He typically spent
three to four hours in an outdoor painting session, sometimes
returning to the site a half-dozen times (weather permitting)
before being satisfied that he had captured what he needed for
future development. Since he might not develop the sketch into a
full-size painting until months later, his memory of factual details,
weather, and visual effects was of great help.

In the early 1980s Koestner began making three or four solo excursions a year from Nininger. These were spring, summer, and fall trips into southeastern Minnesota, western Wisconsin, northwestern Iowa, and eastern Missouri.

One afternoon in Missouri, Koestner was absorbed in sketching a Mississippi River scene near Hannibal. His vantage from a scenic overlook gave him a view east beyond a small farm in a wooded valley to a broad sweep of floodplain—some of it cropland—with the wide, meandering river at its center. It had been a beautiful day until a wind suddenly arose and the sky clouded up. A couple stopping to admire the view mentioned the radio report of a severe thunderstorm moving into the area. As a precaution, Koestner took down the metal rod that supported his umbrella rig and put the apparatus in the car, then returned to his painting. The oil sketch was going well, and he wanted to capture as much as he could before packing up for the day. A few moments later he was jarred by an ear-cracking explosion of lightning, and the heavy metal guardrail that he stood behind "twanged like a guitar string." Driving back to the motel, happy to be alive, the artist remembered seeing "some beautiful cloud effects."

Like all landscape painters, Koestner sometimes found himself in adverse weather. He wasn't reckless, having learned from experience to be attentive to Mother Nature's occasional rages. But working alone and often out of sight of others, he was vulnerable—especially when on rocky, unstable terrain or in conditions of extreme heat or cold. Still, the joys of painting out of doors far outnumbered the pitfalls.

Koestner found the outdoors a stimulating work environment in all seasons, but he cautioned his students that a landscape painter had to have an eye even greater than a farmer's for the weather. He described Minnesota winter conditions in an essay on landscape painting:

In my north country, painting a winter landscape outside poses a particular challenge. Even with today's efficient cold-weather clothing, one has to put on as many layers as possible, for the cold penetrates much more when one is standing still for a couple of hours than it does when one is active in subzero weather. Here again, wind is the prime enemy. I have worked in temperatures as low as 15 degrees below zero on calm days, but have had to give up at 30 degrees above because of wind. I use snowshoes to get to my [painting site], and stand on them while painting, for they keep my boots from direct contact with the cold snow. Dressed as warmly as necessary, [I have the] problem of becoming overheated if I have to trek very far. Because of this, I have never gone more than a quarter mile from the car, house, or cabin. It is necessary to mix a few drops of kerosene with each mound of paint on the palette. Without this, the oil paint becomes too stiff to allow brushing.

One winter day, Koestner worked on location longer than he should have. When he returned the quarter mile or so to his car his fingers were so numb that he couldn't turn the ignition key. Fumbling through the car's emergency toolbox, he found some pliers and clumsily grasped them to turn the key and start the car for the drive home.

Weather requires a painter's constant attention because it brings changing light conditions. Once a painting is in its middle stages (with composition established and important shapes blocked in), work can proceed only when the weather cooperates. A persistence of cloudy days when the scene requires sunshine stalls production. To portray uncommon effects such as fog, moving water, or passing cloud shadows, Koestner waited for days, weeks, and sometimes years to get enough days of correct condition to complete a painting. The problem compounded in spring or fall when seasonal changes offer a limited number of sessions on any single work. To keep busy, he usually had several works in progress at the same time. To increase his chances of finding at least one part of the day with suitable light, his works-in-progress were typically morning, afternoon, and evening scenes.

Nature is Koestner's church, and in painting outdoors, he says, he felt "an intensity and vigor seldom approached in the studio." In a lecture, *Nature*, Ralph Waldo Emerson described the experience: "In the presence of nature a wild delight runs through the man . . . . In the woods, we return to reason and faith. . . . In the tranquil landscape, and especially in the distant line of the horizon, man beholds something as beautiful as his own nature."

Writer John Gardner observed a similar revelation in his novel *October Light:* "He saw how the stones and grass of the pasture turned spiritual in this light, radiating power, as if charged with some old, mystic energy."

"Light," Koestner says, "is the subject of my paintings." Writing about it, he described his aim: "A prevalent notion is that the artist's sole motivation is to portray a particular scene with as photographic a verisimilitude as possible. But to the painter, the inspiration for the work may lie entirely in what the sun does to that scene at a particular time of day and season. It is a complex phenomenon."

Painting in nature requires a high tolerance for discomfort. Sudden wind gusts can pick up a canvas and sail it into the next township; gnats and black flies bite the neck and crawl up the pant legs. It is all part of the day's work, Koestner told his students. Some who visited his home on summer weekends to try their hand at outdoor painting arrived unprepared, wearing shorts, sandals, and short-sleeved shirts more appropriate for a picnic in a city park. Novice painters quickly became aware not only of brambles and bugs but also of the immensity of the landscape around them. What to paint? Where are the boundaries? Where to begin? It took awhile for them to select a small slice of nature's feast and block out the rest. Believing that landscape painters are called to their vocation, Koestner stops short of encouraging anyone to pursue this form of painting. He believes that dedicated landscape painters "are born, not made." He considers them "a breed apart" from those pursuing portrait and genre painting. He says they have tended to be more independent, less associated with academies and teaching, less bound by rules than their contemporaries in other branches of painting.

Koestner's influences in his long road to becoming an accomplished landscape painter have included at least a dozen painters— all from the nineteenth and early twentieth centuries: John Constable, J. M. W. Turner, Jean-Baptiste-Camille Corot, Claude Monet, Charles-Francois Daubigny, Martin Johnson Heade, Childe Hassam, George Inness, Thomas Moran, Frederick Church, Sanford Gifford, and Worthington Whitridge. Their styles—romantic, realist, impressionist— varied but all painted outdoors in the vastness of a natural world of changing light and color, of rustling leaves, of rippling streams and billowing clouds.

Koestner's discovery of the works of George Inness in the Edward B. Butler collection of the Art Institute of Chicago provided his greatest early influence. Inness, an American painter who died in 1894, was a maverick often out of favor with art critics of his time, an artist less influenced than most by popular tastes and trends.

"Inness's paintings seemed magical to me in their evocative power while also retaining a look of truth," Koestner said. "Though I have come to recognize his shortcomings, I still look to Inness as an ideal of expression in landscape painting."

In Koestner's studies of these artist's works in museum collections, he noted how their styles evolved over their lifetimes, that they were not static: "They followed their own path." Decades after completing art school, he felt that his style—part realism, part impressionism—was also still evolving.

"I don't think I've gone beyond impressionism," Koestner said, "but I have combined it with other techniques such as glazing [putting liquid dark paint over light] and scumbling [putting liquid light paint over dark], which I've picked up from Gifford, Turner, Moran, and Inness."

From a painter's viewpoint, both form and color appear different in sunlight than they do on cloudy days or in the north light of the studio window. The French impressionists preferred sunlight but found it limited a working session to perhaps two hours due to constantly changing light and shadow shapes. This required the artists to work quickly, with loose strokes of the brush, to capture the color and tone of what they saw. They were less concerned with an object's detail than with the scene's overall light effect, or impression.

Koestner's move toward impressionism was gradual. He studied the works of Monet, particularly, inspecting the paintings close up to see Monet's buildup of paint color—so close that museum guards, concerned about picture damage, sometimes tapped him on the shoulder. In his reading about technical aspects of painting Koestner learned that the impressionists had applied "pure color" touches of opposing hues side by side on their canvases. These, when seen at a distance, were blended by the viewer's eye.

"At first, that had no concrete meaning to me," Koestner said, "It did not seem to jibe with what I observed on the surface of paintings labeled 'impressionist.'" He said he didn't fully grasp impressionist technique until discovering *Landscape Painting*, a book by Birge Harrison.

Harrison wrote: "Colors dance, but values stay put."

Koestner was astounded by the simplicity of it all: "I suddenly perceived that the scintillating color effects I had enjoyed in impressionist paintings were the result of a close understanding of the use of values within a given color area. Though the painter might juxtapose opposing hues in a sky, for example, each of the separate hues was carefully mixed with white on the palette so that their values were identical. With this revelation, I began applying broken-color technique in my paintings in an effort to enhance that vibration of color that is apparent in nature."

Koestner occasionally uses a camera as an aid to record scenes or special effects. He acknowledges that photography has "a legitimate and useful place" in the production of landscape paintings. The medium, he says, was used more than generally realized by many accomplished painters in the late nineteenth century—"but as an adjunct for knowledge, not a substitute."

He expanded on the topic in an essay on landscape painting: "There is a difference between the occasional use of a photographic aid by an accomplished painter and the almost total reliance on their use by many contemporary artists who produce works that fall under the category of traditional art [examples are southwest art and wildlife art]. We have all been subjected to the photographic image that the public, and many artists, equate with visual reality. In fact, the eye perceives things differently from the way a camera records them. Looking at a tree, for instance, the eye sees a mass of color and value shapes, whereas the camera records every leaf. Furthermore, photos generally distort value, color, and perspective."

The "filtering of the subject through the mind" is also lost in the mechanical image of the photographic print. Koestner wrote: "Pencil sketches and notation require more time, but they provide the artist with a much more lasting impression and memory of the thing observed than the flat image obtained by merely looking through the viewfinder and clicking the shutter. That subjective impression finds its way into a painting and can be seen and appreciated by others."

"I am not a painter to be watched," Koestner said, and usually refused requests to do painting demonstrations. "My paintings are built up slowly, the final painting containing many layers."

Preferring to work unnoticed and undisturbed, Koestner has not always been able to isolate himself from curious passersby. Dressed in work clothes, a visor cap on his head, he appears approachable—he is not an eccentric who might snarl or snap at a question. But his affability has sometimes been abused, as happened one morning when a tourist stopped to see what he was painting. The man glanced at the canvas, then rudely stepped in front of Koestner's easel with his camera to capture his own rendition of the panoramic scene. "Got it!" the intruder said. "Took *me* less than a minute."

Another time, while he was doing an outdoor oil sketch at a Pennsylvania coal town, several youngsters approached him. One asked, "Are you a real artist or are you doing this just for fun?"

"Both," Koestner replied.

In a brochure for a show at Kilbride-Bradley Gallery in the 1960s, Koestner's friend and associate Richard Lack already compared him to the nineteenth century American impressionist George Inness: "As in the work of this predecessor, Koestner views the world with the eye of the poet, quick to respond to those effects of nature which embody harmony, tranquility, and solitude. This is not an artist who 'copies what he sees' in the derogatory modern sense, but rather a highly sensitive eye that uses the faculty of selection to achieve not imitation but art. Here, familiar to all of us, are the rolling vistas of our state—farmhouses and granaries, clouds and water, prairie evenings and starlit nights."

Photo Section II

Lorna and Fred ages six and seven.

Above right: Half-mile gravel road from Koestner home in the woods to fields beyond, 1970s.

Left: Don Koestner viewing nature with customary concentration, June 1971.

Below: Don Koestner in his Nininger living room, late 1970s.

Top: Koestner cabin near Silver Bay on Lake Superior. The family began spending summers there in 1969.

Above left: Don's homemade ladder provides access to beach about 40 feet below cliff.

Above right: Wooden rig for drawing water from the lake, one pail at a time.

Right: Fred, 6, and Lorna, 5, explore the beach.

Above: Koestner's 1970 painting of their North Shore cliff showing ladder to beach. Fern descending ladder; Fred scaling wall below; Lorna on beach.

Below and right: Three photos of Lake Superior from the Koestner property. The stone arch *(lower right)* became a favorite subject of the painter.

Don built a roofed platform near the edge of the cliff and there did several paintings of Fern.

Left: Don decides where Fern and the children are to pose in this 1972 photo.

Below: Don's painting set-up in front of the platform. While the models take a break, Lorna and Fred are joined by family friend, Vicky Hakala.

Left: Richard Lack and Don Koestner "talk shop," 1985. Stone arch in background.

Don Koestner teaching portrait class at the Minnesota Museum Art School, St. Paul, 1974.

Painter friends gather at Koestner show at Master Framers, St. Paul, 1980s.

Left: Richard Lack.

Below: Don Koestner and Mike Coyle.

Paul Van Demark and Don Koestner.

Right: Don Koestner and Katherine Lack at party for Koestners, 1986, prior to the Koestners' move to Silver Bay.

Don and Fern examine an oversized, hand-made greeting card signed by friends.

Right: Cliff Moen.

The Koestners' move to Silver Bay in 1986 required them to remodel and expand the summer cabin built in 1969. The expansion project began by temporarily moving the cabin onto skids to make way for excavation and construction of a full basement. The cabin was jacked up, then pushed onto the skids with a Caterpillar tractor. Many of the hired laborers were Silver Bay neighbors.

Left: Excavated hole for new addition with several tiers of concrete block already in place. In the background is the Koestner cabin, temporarily relocated to make room for construction of basement.

Lower left: Delivery of more blocks to build basement walls.

Below: Basement nearly completed, except for poured concrete floor.

Cabin being pushed toward the new foundation by "Cat" operator Ken Drowley (right). Don Koestner (left) directs maneuver. (Ribbons on walls discourage woodpeckers.)

The move is complete.

Work crew at end of day. Left to right: Cam Torgerson, Dawson Usack (and son Todd), Ken Drowley, Don Koestner, Sep Reger, and Roy Ranum.

Installing floor joists for studio and bedroom addition, east of original cabin.

Above: Silver Bay neighbors frame and sheath the addition. Carl "Herc" Roebin with circular saw.

Below: The nearly completed addition, with studio skylight in place.

Above: North side of cabin, with addition of enclosed entry. Siding being applied.

Below left: Fern sweeps her new porch and steps.

Below right: Don and Fern move in.

Top: North view of completed home, re-roofed, sided and freshly painted.

Right: Fern and Don open gifts from neighbors at their open house. At right, Maria Drowley.

Below: Silver Bay neighbors celebrate with Koestners. From left: Maria and Ken Drowley, Genalda Ranum, Dee Torgerson, and Evie Buetow.

Top: South view of Koestner home near Silver Bay.

Left: View of living room.

Below left: Don in new studio.

Below right: Compact kitchen table, with two space-saving, swing-out stools designed and built by Don.

Above: Fern Koestner, left, and gallery visitor at Don Koestner's one-man show at Heritage Gallery in Alexandria, Virginia, 1987. Behind them, Don's *Autumn Sunset.*

Right: A corner of the gallery lined with Koestner paintings.

Below: Fern and Don stand beside *Early Morning Autumn* at Minnesota River School of Art, Bloomington, Minnesota, 1990s.

In his Studio

Koestner poses for a *Hastings Star* profile,
June 1979.

Grinding pigment, 1985,
Nininger studio.

Right: Koestner studio, 2001,
Silver Bay, Minnesota.

Work tables, paint tubes, rags, brushes, studio mirror and other supplies and furnishings of the painter's craft.

Painting Outdoors

Koestner paints on rural road
near Nininger, 1960s.

Painting on Lake Superior shore.

Painting in Finland State Forest, north
of Silver Bay, 1992. Photo by Franz
Ulrich.

Koestner paints west of Silver Bay, near Tettagouche State Park.

Koestner on rock ledge at mouth of the Beaver River, Lake Superior, 1997.
Photo by Richard Colburn.

Koestner works on oil sketch near Balltown, Iowa, September 2004 (four months after Fern's death and two months before his 81st birthday).

In 1993, Don Koestner (left, on ladder) helped his daughter, Lorna (in window), build a log cabin on land she bought near Carlton, Minnesota, south of Duluth. The logs are from pine trees cut on her 40-acre parcel. She moved them into position using a farm tractor with a front-end loader she had acquired second hand. (Don was not Lorna's only helper on this labor-intensive construction project.)

A book featuring Koestner's work, *Don Koestner: American Impressionist*, was published in November 2005 and promoted at a book-signing party held at The Atelier Studio Program of Fine Art in Minneapolis. The large format book includes 135 paintings, plus a short biography and artist's notes on painting craft. Koestner inscribed more than 200 copies of the book.

Above left: Standing behind the artist is Annette LeSueur, who, with Mike Coyle, initiated the art-book project and organized the book-signing event.

Above right: Koestner signs book for a patron.

Below: Guests mingle near the buffet table, left.

Speaking to Don Koestner are Franz Ulrich, left, and Lisa Bormann, center.

Koestner stands with producers of *Don Koestner: American Impressionist*.
From left, Mike Coyle and Annette LeSueur; Vicky and Bill Hakala.

Beside Don Koestner are Cyd Wicker, left, and Dale Redpath, right, who direct The Atelier, a school dedicated to training traditional painters.

Fred Koestner (Don's son) with wife, Dawn, and their son, Benjamin.

Left: Lorna Koestner with two garden treasures, August 2007.

Center: Lorna's son, Justin, on shore of Lake Superior, March 2007. (Don Koestner's property in background.)

Below: Technicians from Rural Renewable Energy Alliance, Ryan Matthews and Charles Krysel, install solar hot-water panels on south-facing roof of Koestner's home in September 2007. Don commissioned the installation when his 20-year-old hot-water heater needed replacement. The conservation-minded artist seized the opportunity to convert his hot-water heat source from propane to solar energy as "an investment in the future."

I am I plus my surroundings;
and if I do not preserve the latter,
I do not preserve myself.

Jose Ortega y Gasset

Silver Bay

IN 1985, DON AND FERN THOUGHT ABOUT MOVING to the North Shore to live there full time. Several changes prompted the consideration. First, Nininger was no longer the rural community it had been in the 1950s, its farm fields and sparse settlement giving way to housing developments as the city of Hastings expanded northward along the river bluff. Painting opportunities in the area had become scarce, and Koestner drove farther from home each year to find suitable landscape subjects. Another factor was his age. In November he would turn 62 and become eligible for early Social Security benefits; he could draw his pension in Silver Bay as well as in Nininger. Their children's independence also played into the prospect of a move. Both had graduated from Hastings High School: Fred in 1981, Lorna in 1983. Fred lived at home but, as a field service technician, frequently traveled. Lorna was in her second year of college in Iowa and could spend summers with them at Silver Bay.

That September, Don and Fern stayed at the cabin later than usual. One day, hiking up a steep, rocky trail in Tettegouche State Park to explore painting sites, Don felt a gnawing ache in his shoulders—first left, then right. Aware of angina symptoms from an earlier episode that had resolved itself, he ignored it. In October, climbing a hill when painting between Prescott and Diamond Bluff on the Wisconsin side of the Mississippi, he felt a similar sensation. Again, the feeling passed.

One evening a few weeks later, having spent an hour or so during the day cutting wood with his chainsaw, Don got another ache in his upper arms, and this time it wouldn't go away. Fern called a physician who owned several Koestner paintings and, acting on the doctor's recommendation, drove Don from Nininger to United Hospital in St. Paul. There, the physician determined he had suffered a mild heart attack. When they recommended a bypass operation, Don told them his insurance wouldn't cover it. The next morning he was transferred to Veterans Medical Center, not far from the Minneapolis neighborhoods where he had lived during the 1930s and 1940s.

The service at the overburdened VA hospital was not what Koestner had experienced at United. Don and Fern sat for several hours in the waiting room, without breakfast or much sleep the night before, before anyone came to attend him. After Don got into a wheelchair, he fainted. Later, alone in his hospital room, the seriousness of his condition—especially the potential loss of his ability to paint—weighed on him for the first time. But the triple-bypass surgery, correcting two narrowed arteries and one blocked artery, went well. On his dismissal, the medical staff told him he was an "exemplary patient."

Released the day after Thanksgiving, Don rode with Fern to the Minneapolis Institute of Arts to see a touring exhibition of George Inness paintings. A painter friend, Wayne Howell, met them there to push Don's wheelchair through the familiar galleries. He made a second visit to the institute a few weeks later, to review the show for the spring 1986 issue of *Classical Realism Quarterly*, published by the Classical Realism Society in Minneapolis. His critique reflected his high regard for the nineteenth-century artist whose works he had studied for years in the Edward B. Butler Collection at the Art Institute of Chicago. Although disheartened by the condition of the century-old masterpieces in the show—a restorer had stripped away glazes along with the top varnish coat—Don wrote admiringly of Inness:

> This major retrospective makes it apparent that Inness was perhaps the foremost American landscape painter; in his best works, he remains unsurpassed in this art by the painters of any time or country. He applied to landscape painting the Venetian method of glazing and scumbling, while yet retaining truth of color and natural effect. In this technique, he was equal if not superior to [Joseph Mallord William] Turner or Thomas Moran. Particularly in his later works, the surfaces are a delight to the gourmet of paint handling; some are achieved in a deceptively simple manner. There is a broadness and unity in his pictures that strongly convey a feeling of truth to nature.

By the spring of 1986, Don had recovered enough from his bypass surgery to begin developing plans for a full-time home at Silver Bay. It was to include a basement, septic system, and a combination wood-and-propane-burning furnace. Excavation and construction of the basement began in June. To position the foundation so that the house faced directly south, Koestner set a pole in the ground and observed its shadow at noon. The core structure would be the original cabin built in 1968, located a few dozen yards east of the new foundation.

Don and Fern thought they would have to hire a house mover from Duluth to move the cabin onto the new foundation, but the Koestner luck bloomed again when Don sought out his closest neighbor, Ken Drowley, for a recommendation. "I can do that with my 'Cat,'" Drowley said. With his bulldozer, Drowley also excavated a hole for the basement. He recommended a friend, Mel Nicklason, to do the concrete work.

"Mel Nicklason was a great find," Don says. Nicklason was a tireless worker, despite a limp caused by years of troweling cement on his knees. "He engineered the whole basement from the plans I had made and was often on the job at 5 A.M., working until dusk." Nicklason's husky son-in-law laid cement blocks for the basement walls.

All of the men in the Koestners' close-knit neighborhood were Reserve Mining Company workers, laid off when the taconite processing operation closed in July following the bankruptcy of LTV Steel, a co-owner of Reserve Mining. Reserve had fought a long battle in federal district court over its practice of discharging wastes into Lake Superior (the plant opened in 1955, and after 1964 it was dumping 67,000 tons of waste a day as a cost-saving practice). Public concern arose when asbestos fibers found in the wastes raised health concerns among lakeshore residents. Under pressure, in 1980 Reserve built a $375 million air-filtering system and an on-land disposal site north of the lake, and ceased dumping in the lake. Company publicists called it "the largest and costliest single pollution-control project in American history."

Fern wrote Mel Nicklason a check every week but had to force money on Ken Drowley for his work. "I got nothing else to do," Drowley said. He was on his bulldozer virtually every day, maneuvering the huge machine with skill and precision. He pushed the cabin onto its new foundation, set the 800-gallon plastic tank that Koestner bought to contain water pumped from the lake, and placed it on a rock ledge on the south side of the house. He later pushed dirt fill around it with his bulldozer. Once the cabin was on its new base, another laid-off mine worker from Silver Bay, Carl "Herc" Roebin, built a 20-by-22-foot addition on the southeast side of the cabin. Koestner handled some of the finishing work on the inside.

The Koestners' neighbors along the shore had 200-foot-deep wells, most of which had required several drillings through the rock before water was found, adding to the cost. Worse, their wells had a salty taste. Koestner preferred to draw his water from Lake Superior as he had for the past 18 summers. It was soft water, drinkable once it was filtered at the faucet. Getting the water from lake to cistern, however, required more innovative engineering.

Years earlier, Koestner had devised a relatively simple crank-and-pulley system attached to a wooden framework anchored securely on the bluff. Now, Koestner had Ken Drowley construct and install a stronger and more permanent metal framework, based on the wooden model. Using a boat-trailer winch, Koestner could lower into the lake a two-inch diameter hose, on the end of which was an electric-powered, submersible pump. Atop the bluff the hose extended 220 feet to the buried cistern near the house. An electric cable ran alongside the hose from the bluff to the house-power supply. No more hauling buckets. To protect the submersible pump from rocks tossed about in the waves, Larry Rasmussen, one of Koestner's helpers, enclosed it in a short length of six-inch diameter pipe with a wire screen at the bottom to filter out sand and other small particles. Another pump, in the basement, drew water from the cistern into a pressure tank that provided the kitchen and bath with water. Thereafter, Koestner pumped water from the lake year-round, though in stormy weather the submersible pump sometimes clogged with sand. The couple's cooking, cleaning, and bathing needs required refilling the cistern every two or three weeks. Ideal conditions for his bimonthly pumping operation were days with little wind so in summer the lake was calm and in winter free of shore ice. Once a pumping operation was completed, the pump was cranked out of the water to the top of the cliff where it was secured in a weathertight shed. The shed's floor was the original cabin door, made of drift plywood salvaged from the Mississippi River. Koestner used other plywood remnants for the shed's sides and roof.

—⁓—

THE KOESTNERS CONVERTED THE SILVER BAY CABIN to a year-round home with funds from the sale of the Nininger property. In June 1986, they sold the house and 4.5 acres to a developer who already owned 30 acres of adjoining land. The Koestners' sale price of $60,000—Don thought it a reasonable return on his $500 payment to Captain Jeremy for the land in 1950—provided him with more than enough money to construct a year-round home in Silver Bay. The buyer allowed the Koestners to continue using their Nininger house until they moved in the fall.

The move to Silver Bay was scheduled to begin Labor Day weekend. Fern described what became a harrowing event in a letter to her sister, Becky Bauman, as "the worst 24 hours of my life." Moving is a daunting task under the best of conditions, but the Koestners' ordeal was made worse by having a surprise renter move into the Nininger house the day after Labor Day. Fern assumed they had the first two weeks of September to clear out their belongings, but without their knowledge the new owner had rented the house to a woman whose children would start school on the Tuesday following Labor Day. The young family had to get settled over the weekend.

The unanticipated demand on the Koestners to vacate their home quickly was made still more difficult when they discovered that U-Haul trucks were all spoken for over the back-to-college weekend. In a state of near panic, they borrowed a broken-down truck and horse trailer from a friend of a friend. The trailer, parked in a field overgrown with thistle, was filled with rotting hay bales and old newspapers. These had to be cleaned out, a broken hitch repaired, tires filled, and a gas leak repaired on the truck. The trailer lacked working taillights, so Koestner duct-taped a red cloth over a flashlight lens and wired that to the side of the trailer.

The loan of a second truck eased their dilemma somewhat. A driver who dropped off their laundered carpets on Friday volunteered his van; he wouldn't need it over the holiday weekend.

Driving two vehicles, Don and Fern left Hastings about dusk for the roughly 200-mile trip to Silver Bay. It was past midnight when they finally dropped into bed. Twin Cities friends Mike Coyle and Wayne Howell had promised to be at the house by 8 A.M. to help with unloading. Fern rummaged in the van where she had put the alarm clock and set it for 6 A.M.; after a hasty breakfast they started unloading. Coyle and Howell arrived on time, and with their help the Koestners completed the job before noon. The crew then headed to Castle Danger, where friends Char and Seth Tidbal had promised to furnish a lunch.

Refreshed, Fern and Don resumed their journey south to the Twin Cities. About halfway, Don, driving ahead of Fern with the truck and trailer, fell asleep and to Fern's horror turned off the road and down a slight embankment. The jar yanked Don awake. Grinning at Fern as she drove by, he pulled back onto the highway.

Fern stopped beside the road, fearful of continuing. Don pulled up behind her and said, "I'm okay, I've had my nap."

Back in Nininger on Monday night after returning the borrowed vehicles, Don and Fern discovered that the renter had jammed whatever they had not yet removed into 10 large plastic garbage bags and set them out for the garbage collector. On top of one sack were several bath towels and Don's bevel-edged, plate-glass, studio mirror. Fern's sympathetic feelings for the young mother's plight "evaporated rapidly."

"Mad! I was so angry, I'll tell you!" Fern wrote to her sister. "I had to quietly let [the renter] know I was *very* unhappy about the way things were going."

The Koestners stuffed the bags into their two cars and hauled them north to sort through later, but it took years to discover what was missing. Items suddenly remembered but not seen since the move included an old sketchbook with a drawing Don made in 1944 of the hillside city of Oran, Algeria, sketched from the deck of his troopship on the Mediterranean.

By late November 1986, the Koestners were settled into their new home. The house was smaller than their Nininger place, but it had a basement, a loft for an extra bed and storage, and a studio with north light. On Thanksgiving, the North Shore temperature was unusually warm at 45 degrees F. and Koestner spent several hours on an outdoor oil sketch.

Don had bought a snow thrower the winter before his heart attack, and Fred used it at Nininger to keep their long driveway clear. Don brought it up to Silver Bay but found it would not work on the gravel driveway. Thanks to another good neighbor, Cam Torgerson, he didn't need it. The retired mine worker said he would keep the driveway free of snow with his homemade log skidder, a practice he continues. He also had installed Koestner's furnace and hot-water heater and cut and delivered a winter supply of firewood, a practice he also continues.

A distinctive feature of the Koestners' new home was its heating system, a furnace in the basement that could be regulated to run on either wood or propane: propane for the warmer fall and spring season and during absences from home, wood when outside temperatures fell below 30 degrees F. For their first North Shore winter, Don stockpiled a half-dozen cords of firewood. Torgerson dumped the split logs on the north side of the house near a basement window, through which Koestner could restock his basement supply as needed. In November, still in recovery from heart surgery, Don had to be careful about lifting, so Fern helped transfer the wood into the basement.

Don and Fern were saddened when the developer who bought their Nininger property razed the house to prepare the site for construction of several large homes. Although the structure was old and in need of repair, Don felt it had "good use in it yet," and its destruction—the local fire department burned it—seemed wasteful to him. For Fern and the children, imagining the house reduced to ashes was heart-wrenching. Fern had lived in Nininger for 26 years, longer than she had lived in any other place. She had helped plan the expansion and made it a comfortable home, hung curtains, organized bookshelves, cupboards and closets, cooked and cleaned, and raised her children there. For Fred and Lorna the house and property represented their childhood landscape, a permanent imprint.

For Don Koestner, though inclined to "live in the present and not look back," the house in the woods represented 36 years of his life. It embodied his quest to become a painter, his independence, his cabin building with materials scavenged from the river, his courtship and marriage, and friendships with local people who had accepted him into their rural community as the "artist of Nininger."

The eye sees what it has the means of seeing,
and its means of seeing are in proportion
to the love and desire behind it.

John Burroughs

New Horizons

CHANCE PLAYED A VITAL ROLE in Don Koestner's discovery of subject matter. At times it was almost as if the subject—a pond at sunset, a birch grove in early morning light, an abandoned farmstead—found him. As he drove or walked, he was alert to these moments of connection. To develop the impression into a successful painting, however, could take years.

In August 1982, a few years before their permanent move to Silver Bay, Don and Fern drove north to Ontario to escape two weeks of rain at the cabin, only to find it still raining on their return. They headed home to Nininger for a few days. Their timing, it turned out, was perfect. Driving south from Superior along

Wisconsin 35, a route Don favored over Minnesota's I-35 from Duluth, he witnessed "one of the most spectacular thunderhead-cloud skies I have ever seen." Looking east, he saw a landscape suspended between turbulence and tranquility. Glowing golden in the foreground was a scattering of hay bales in a mowed field. But behind him was a white cumulus cloud billowing against a backdrop of flatter, windswept clouds that the setting sun colored yellow and orange. The sky was a mottled blue—beautiful yet threatening. Coincidentally, the site of this chance encounter with the developing storm was the village of Luck. In a letter to a friend, Anna Van Demark Quinn, Don described how he captured the impression:

> I made some notes [on the cloud formations] and also observed a nice farm landscape that I could put with the sky. The next day I did a memory color sketch of the sky and went up in the afternoon to do a drawing of the farm buildings and landscape. I now have a 36-by-49-inch canvas going based on this information. I went back to Luck with the canvas and worked an evening, mostly on the farm buildings. Since, I've built up some textures (mostly in reds) on the rest of the landscape elements. I'm enthused about this painting. Whether I will be able to bring it off or not remains to be seen, but anyway I've now got a project to work on in the studio at the cabin if the weather remains bad there.

Don completed *Evening Thunderheads* four years later, in 1986. The large painting was one of dozens that he had in his studio for development on rainy days and during winter months.

Through most of the preceding seven or eight years Fern's earnings from photo retouching—roughly $3,500 a year—exceeded Don's income from painting sales. He was always painting, so his meager income did not reflect his productivity. He exhibited his work wherever a decent gallery showed an interest. Few did. His was a dilemma faced by most traditional painters: opportunities to exhibit and sell their work were limited, publicity rare, audiences small.

Since 1970, Don had participated in dozens of shows. One of the most successful was a one-man show at the Gallery Upstairs in Hastings. Gallery owners Bertrand and Margaret Goderstad operated a clothing store, "The Clothes Buggy," below. More than 200 invited guests viewed the exhibit at its gala opening on October 15, 1971. A part of the show's attraction was the gallery's location on the old river town's historic main street. Don showed 50 paintings, selling a dozen during its three-week run. Fern kept a record of every painting sold, and to whom.

Don Koestner had a number of other one-man shows during this period: St. Paul's Osborne Gallery in 1976, the Croft near Hastings (1977 and 1979), and St. Paul's Master Framers in 1984. He also participated in group shows such as one held at the Wyer-Pierce Art Gallery in Minneapolis in 1982. There he sold the last still life he would ever do. He painted still lifes with a master's touch, but the meticulous execution of static objects in a controlled studio setting lacked for him the emotional excitement and challenge of working in nature. His work was also part of a group touring show that went to museums in the states of Washington, Utah, and Texas.

At a show at the Minnetonka Art Center (a western suburb of Minneapolis) in 1982, Koestner sold several large landscapes, one from oil sketches done in Missouri and two that he had painted along the Upper Mississippi near Wabasha and Winona. At the time, his prices ranged from $500 to $2,000, depending on the oil sketch or painting.

Koestner's painting sales rose unexpectedly in September 1985 with the opening of a new gallery—one committed to the work of traditional painters. The gallery promised to be a boon to those largely ignored by an art establishment of schools, colleges, galleries, and critics favoring modernist works.

The Heritage Art Gallery was the brainchild of Peggy Yarborough, a Georgia native studying at Atelier LeSueur in Minnetonka, Minnesota. Earlier, in high school, Yarborough had ached to learn the fundamentals of art, but she found no instruction except through a Famous Artists correspondence course. Later, in art classes at the University of Georgia, instructors and classmates ridiculed her careful drawings as "out of touch."

Yarborough eventually traveled to Minneapolis, hoping Richard Lack might accept her as a student. Lack, not taking any new students at the time, recommended her to Annette LeSueur (leh-SWARE), a former Lack student now operating her own studio school. There, Yarborough began to wonder why the dedicated and accomplished painters she came to know in the Twin Cities got such little notice. It seemed to her that their masterworks, when rarely exhibited, were underpriced. Did no one appreciate the training and effort that went into a well-crafted work of art?

Yarborough began thinking about the potential of a gallery that exhibited traditional painting exclusively, one that not only showed the work but also educated the public about the deep heritage and craft of painting. Such a gallery might showcase traditional painters working in many areas of the country.

In a chance encounter with Richard Lack at a shopping center one day, she shared her idea of starting a gallery. He immediately expressed interest. When she asked him how many traditional painters he knew across the United States, Lack said "at least 40" —and he could provide names and addresses.

Location was critical to Yarborough. She doubted that such a gallery could thrive in the Twin Cities, despite the community's support of other traditional art forms: a world-class symphony orchestra, the nation's only full-time professional chamber music orchestra, and a renowned theater with a classical repertoire of plays.

Yarborough ultimately selected Alexandria, Virginia, for her gallery. Adjacent to Washington, D.C., the city was an international crossroads visited by people from around the world. She had worked in Washington and knew its potential.

A friend, Jack Lynch, agreed to finance the gallery start-up. A successful Virginia real estate developer, Lynch leased a building on Alexandria's historic Lloyd's Row. The one-story site had about 3,000 square feet of space divided among five large rooms, and Lynch began renovating it to Yarborough's vision for a first-class gallery. One of her priorities was good lighting. The old building lacked skylights, so she worked with lighting engineers to install a cutting-edge system giving the effect of natural light.

To achieve the educational mission of her dream, Yarborough produced a video for gallery visitors about the growing but largely unnoticed underground movement of traditional painters working across the country. It included studio interviews with Richard Lack and Don Koestner. This 28-minute presentation, *Awakening of a New Generation*, explained the difference between craft-based traditional painting and what Yarborough termed "fast-food art."

In August 1985, Jack Lynch arrived at Nininger to pick up 33 of Don Koestner's ornately framed paintings for the Alexandria gallery's September opening. As Koestner watched Lynch's bus-size van pull away, he could only hope for good results. The proof was in the sales.

Over the next three years, the Heritage Art Gallery sold nearly a painting a month for Koestner—and at more than his usual prices. In an informed art market, price is an important indicator not only of competency and excellence but also of enduring value and limited supply. The paintings exhibited were original master-pieces painstakingly created on sound principles of composition, drawing, and paint handling. The gallery's price of $7,000 for one Koestner landscape—*The Lone Farm* (the title paid homage to a George Inness landscape)—was the highest his work had com-manded; he received $4,500 from the sale. His total income from the sales at Heritage Art Gallery was nearly $45,000. The unan-ticipated earnings required Koestner to pay back the partial Social Security benefits he had begun drawing at age 62.

Although the gallery's long-term goal of creating a lasting marketplace for traditional painters were never fulfilled—the gallery closed after its third year of operation—it succeeded in providing exposure to dozens of gifted painters. Many were later represented in New York and other galleries made aware of them through the Alexandria gallery's initial success. At an auction to clear out its inventory of paintings in September 1988, the Her-itage Art Gallery sold six more Koestner works (more than any other artist represented in the auction). This sale brought him an additional $18,060.

This windfall of painting sales, coupled with the prospect of Don's collecting full Social Security benefits after he turned 65 in November, emboldened the Koestners to take a fall road trip into the Blue Ridge mountains, an area Don had explored 40 years earlier with his college friend, Cliff Moen. Don and Fern also started annuities at their local bank—investment accounts "for old age." For a time, they drew monthly interest from them, leav-ing the principal intact, but soon they let the earnings accrue as well. They had no desire to change their way of living, and they did not.

Between 1986 through 1993, Koestner sold 70 paintings for a total of $158,000 (averaging about $20,000 a year for the eight-year period). Most of the sales were through Heritage, with Lynch continuing to sell Koestner's work in the Alexandria area even after the gallery had closed. Master Framers, a St. Paul gallery that had a long association with Koestner, also sold eight or nine paintings during this period. Beard Gallery in Minneapolis sold another six. All the paintings were sold at Koestner's new prices. He thought it unfair to Heritage Art Gallery to sell his work elsewhere at a lower cost, and found it gratifying that his higher prices didn't discourage local sales. At the Twin Cities shows, many of the buyers were those who had bought his paintings in the 1960s and 1970s when the price was half or less of what he now charged.

The opening of Heritage Art Gallery in 1985 encouraged Richard Lack and his associates in Minneapolis to launch several projects. One was publication of *Realism in Revolution*. The large-format book, introduced at the gallery opening in Alexandria, included half a dozen four-color reproductions of Koestner paintings, along with his essay, "Landscape Painting: The Artist's Perspective." Eleven other traditional painters contributed essays on topics aimed at defining their work and methods. The book contained, Koestner wrote to a friend, "more sound talk about painting than can be found in any other art book that large."

Another of their initiatives was formation of the American Society of Classical Realism. The nonprofit volunteer group's newsletter, *Classical Realism Quarterly: A Journal of Renewal in the Visual Arts*, was at first offered to subscribers for $10 a year. Then it evolved into a four-color magazine that continued for 20 years. At the start, the journal was funded in part by the R. H. Ives Gammell Studio Trust and by Atelier Lack; later it was supported entirely through subscriptions and gifts. The magazine featured Koestner's work twice, in 1992 and 1996.

The Twin Cities group also launched a series of annual "guild shows" exhibiting the work of qualified traditional painters. These efforts brought a sense of cohesion to the members. For a time, their shows drew increasingly better crowds and received local publicity raising awareness of the artists' works.

—⁓—

AS AN IMPRESSIONIST LANDSCAPE PAINTER, Don Koestner considered himself independent of the realist group whose work was more formalized in style and subject matter. He continued to enjoy his association with fellow painters but said, "I work best alone and prize a degree of anonymity and isolation."

Koestner's long experience, combined with his reflectiveness and empathy, made him a good mentor to young painters. He always shared what he knew, answered technical questions, and offered suggestions and encouragement. He understood the doubts they expressed about their progress and the long-term value of what they did.

One such artist was Anna Van Demark Quinn. Anna was the daughter of the Koestners' friends Carol and Paul Van Demark. Koestner saw Anna grow up, then develop into a painter of considerable skill as a four-year student of Richard Lack. She later married a forestry student at the University of Minnesota. She moved to the small town of Divide, Montana, in the Beaver National Forest, where her husband, Brian, got his first assignment with the U.S. Forest Service. They lived in a beautiful part of the West, but she felt cut off. Isolated from the art and cultural-support community she had known most of her life, she surrounded herself with art books. "Carloads of books," her husband said. Brian called her "Anna of the Mountains" because of her daily sketching treks into the wilderness with her backpack easel. The couple's 105-pound malamute, Raven, always accompanied her.

The Quinns spent 10 years in Montana, moving frequently from one small town to another as Brian was promoted. During much of this period (1982 to 1990), Don Koestner corresponded with the couple. In his letters, he responded to Anna's questions and offered her advice and encouragement. Addressing the concerns she expressed about her ability and progress, he described the ups and downs of his own painting projects and work routines. The letters reflect his views on painting craft, on art as a vocation, and on his productivity.

On working alone (Koestner wrote): "The questionings and self-doubts you feel only emphasize your genuineness as a painter . . . I can state as a quite reliable fact for myself that enforced periods of not painting because of frame-making, carpentry work, back trouble, etc., are followed by renewed spurts in which I feel I am painting better than I was before. I feel, in fact, that periods away from painting are really necessary for me. I get depressed, though, and hard to live with if I go too long unable to paint."

On success: "We are much too concerned today with the idea of being "successful". . . I think it is good to periodically define one's purpose to oneself, and once that purpose is defined to pursue it and to hell with what others may think."

On chasing the sun: "Was able to work Sunday afternoon under milky light, and set up at 5:45 to work on my evening thing. Had about 10 minutes of sunshine, and then clouds. I diddled at the painting until 6:45 and then gave up. The sun came out again at 6:55 after I was all packed up. Thus ended a typical landscape painter's day."

An art history lesson: "I was interested in your comments about the Hudson River School as opposed to impressionist paintings. For all the rhapsodic talk by present-day art writers about the impressionists portraying light, there is generally a more true feeling of light in the work of those other schools. I think the impressionists have taught us a fuller use of color, but the techniques, values, and, above all, designing of those others can perhaps teach us more. One of the artists I like, pigeonholed these days as a "luminist," is Sanford R. Gifford. The thing that puts him in the luminist category is that he, and others of the school, used primarily the glazing-scumbling technique. Inness could as well be labeled luminist, but strangely, [he] is often lumped with the impressionists now."

On winter painting outdoors: "It has been below freezing every night for at least three weeks, the lowest being 24 degrees a couple of nights ago. Thanks to my tent I have been able to finish one outdoor painting. It is a 26 x 32 of our birches and the lake in sunset light . . . In spite of the cold, the lake was completely free of ice until about three days ago. Now it is all white ice for quite a ways out. Anyway, when the lake was open it was steaming a lot and it was that effect I tried to paint."

—⚒—

DON KOESTNER CONTINUED TO TAKE ROAD TRIPS, Fern always with him. A one-man show at the Heritage Gallery in 1987 provided them an opportunity to visit galleries in the nation's capital. On the drive home they visited a major exhibit of paintings by John Singer Sargent at the Art Institute of Chicago. Shows of major nineteenth-century painters continued to energize Don, and seeing their work up close deepened his knowledge.

In October 1988, Don and Fern visited the Blue Ridge Mountains, beginning what became a ritual of late-fall painting trips away from familiar landscapes. They generally drove southeast to West Virginia and Pennsylvania, where they could still find fall colors. Don brought along gesso panels for his oil sketches.

"We hit the fall color just right in the Blue Ridge," he wrote to Anna Quinn. "I'm still enthused over the mountain landscapes

I'm attempting to do from my sketches, but am frustrated by lack of information. I'm doing large paintings, too, which is probably unwise, but the subject just seemed to demand a large scale. The largest is 32-by-48-inches, and the smallest I have going so far is 25-by-37-inches. I'm still planning to do one more that will be 24-by-32 inches."

In the spring of 1989, the Koestners received an unexpected gift from their son, Fred: airline tickets to Europe. Fred, then in his late twenties, traveled a good deal as a field-service technician for a Minnesota-based electronics company with international customers. His gift of airline tickets set the stage for a European adventure that the Koestners would not otherwise have considered.

Though he was a tireless road traveler, Don Koestner had never before taken a commercial airline flight. During the war, he had flown over the Himalayas in a military cargo plane to reach his base in China, and he had accompanied his cousin Art in small planes in the 1950s. But when he went to Europe in 1956, it was by ship. Fern had never flown before.

In her travel diary, Fern Koestner described their flight leaving Minneapolis as "suspended in space . . . the small clusters of lights below us passed so slowly, as if they were the object moving, not us. A big full moon peeked over the gleaming edge of the plane's wing."

When they encountered mild turbulence a few hours into the flight, she noted, the bumpy air was "no worse than frost heaves on Highway 61 at this time of year." She then settled down with a Perry Mason mystery for the long flight to London's Gatwick airport.

For three weeks, the Koestners traveled by train through parts of England, Wales, France, and Spain, stayed in hotels, ate in restaurants, and visited museums. A tongue-in-cheek headline in Fern's diary—"We lived at the Prado"—offered a clue to the trip's primary focus. Their Madrid hotel was six blocks from the famous museum holding a large collection of seventeenth-century Diego Velazquez paintings, including *Maids of Honor*. Velazquez was of special interest to Koestner because of the Spanish painter's unique ability to separate forms with light and shadow—a technique rediscovered by impressionist painters two centuries later.

The Koestners spent 16 days in London—five in the National Gallery, two at the Tate, three at the Victoria and Albert Museum, two at the Wallace Collection, and one each at the Queen's Gallery and Barbican Center. "The Barbican had an exhibit of late Victorian painting with some outstanding paintings by Englishmen I had never heard of," Don wrote to Anna Quinn.

In her diary, Fern noted visiting the National Gallery "more times than I can remember." She sometimes sat and "people watched" for hours while Don roamed the galleries. He reveled in the museum's vast collection of John Constable and J. M. W. Turner paintings. He described the London gallery experience to Anna Quinn:

> We looked at about 2,000 paintings from Van Eyck to the impressionists. I came away with a new appreciation of Constable for one. Saw his best large things at the National Gallery, a room full of smaller paintings and sketches [of Constable] at the Tate, and another room full of sketches at the Victoria and Albert, including a 4-by-6-foot "sketch" for *The Haywain*. Saw about an equal number of Turners including sketches and a number of unfinished paintings. The unfinished things were instructive of his methods, at least in his later years. They looked like abstract expressionist paintings—a lot of paint, some put on with palette knife; large broad color areas, and no form. The form and drawing went over such a color lay-in on his more finished work.

Koestner brought his paint box to Europe but once forgot it on a Madrid subway platform. While he held his shoulder to the open door, Fern leaped out to retrieve the box before the train pulled out. He did some sketching near Vitorio, south of Bilbao, and in Swansea and Cardiff, Wales. While Don and Fern had lunch in Cardiff, Fern exchanged pleasantries with a woman sitting nearby; the woman generously invited Fern home with her for a cup of tea and a warm place to wait for Don while he spent the afternoon sketching. Fern noted her "100-year-old cottage, one of a dozen others in a row, like a line of teeth in a mouth." Another woman the Koestners casually met in Wales invited them to stay at her home in Swansea should they ever return.

—∿—

BEGINNING IN 1994, FERN KEPT A JOURNAL of their fall painting trips. Her entries provide a glimpse into the working life of a landscape painter whose success on any given day is much directed by weather. For example:

> September 30, 1994: Left Silver Bay for a leisurely sketching trip south into Wisconsin and Illinois, stopping first at Master Framers in St. Paul to select frames for three paintings completed during the year, then a few visits with family and friends in the Twin Cities and Hastings . . . Stayed overnight at the Terrace Motel for $38. Not cheap anymore.

At Prescott, they crossed the Mississippi and followed Wisconsin 35 south along the river, through Fern's home territory of Bay City and Maiden Rock, then into hilly Trempealeau County to visit friends, and south to Prairie du Chien. They got a motel room in McGregor, on the Iowa side of the river, and stayed there five days while Don worked on two paintings in Pikes Peak State Park—one location in the morning, another in the afternoon. The park occupied the highest elevation (500 feet) overlooking the Mississippi River.

October 7, 1994: We have been at McGregor, Iowa, for five days, and Don's happy with his painting. Several times in these five days it looked as if he'd get rained out, but each time the weather held off or even gave him a better effect than he expected.

Good painting weather and a low-budget motel with decent food made it "a very satisfactory five days," Fern noted. They next drove to Richland Center, Wisconsin, about 50 miles northeast of McGregor, to look for painting opportunities. Richland Center, the birthplace of Frank Lloyd Wright, was nestled among wooded hills. Over the next five days, Koestner did three oil sketches—scenes he found "around each bend in the road."

October 10, 1994: It seems a pity not to take more advantage of the season and weather. Since we've been gone, this is the first perfect day: sun warm and almost no wind. Yesterday was nearly as bad as the last afternoon in McGregor. Then the wind was so terrific that Don was hanging onto the easel and canvas; even a brick wasn't enough. Nor the tube of white lead he'd [also] used to hold down the easel. How he managed to paint, I don't know. People who use photos to paint from don't know what they're missing!

Their last stop was the Art Institute of Chicago—an annual pilgrimage. The following October they returned there for a traveling Monet exhibit. They had viewed a Monet show there five years earlier, and Don thought it "beyond all expectations," but the 1995 show was even better. It included several of Monet's series paintings—mornings on the Seine River, Rouen Cathedral,

London's Parliament. Also represented were more of the impressionist painter's water-lily paintings than in the previous show. On the way back to Minnesota, Koestner spent a few days sketching on U.S. 20 near Galena, Illinois. The location, just below the brow of a hill, was so windy, Fern noted, it "wiggled his canvas." Then they made a four-day return visit to Richland Center, where every day "dawned foggy, but with sun behind it." Fern was bitten on the thumb by a brown spider, took Benadryl for pain, and held her thumb against a glass of ice water to reduce its swelling. But her husband, she wrote, returned home to Silver Bay "satisfied." He had more than enough sketches to keep busy during the winter.

—⁂—

FERN KOESTNER WAS OUTGOING. She thought of herself as "a generalist, interested in many things." She read books, visited friends in the hospital, worked a few hours a week at the food co-op, and met and did projects with the Silver Bay Friends of the Library. At the library, her "second home," she taught a class in origami, painted kid's faces at Halloween, and helped with twice-a-year book-sale fund-raisers. She also met with the local garden club, volunteered as an election judge and second-grade art teacher, helped a church bible study group to prepare food for funerals, and took occasional extension classes at the University of Minnesota's Duluth campus, once on Irish writers.

"Fern was happiest when with a bunch of people," Don Koestner said.

Fern was a self-described "couch potato," but mindful of her need for exercise, she walked almost every day, usually with Don or a neighbor, sometimes alone. On these walks she mentally noted her sightings of flowers, birds, animals, and weather phenomena, then recorded them in assorted notebooks she labeled "phenology journals" to reflect the cycles of plant and wildlife she observed. Since she always accompanied Don on road trips, the journals became diaries of these excursions as well.

Some samplings from summer and fall 1997:

July 8: Discovered a new flower on my walk up by Drowleys. It has a pure white blossom like a morning glory and is a member of that family. It doesn't open up if it is cloudy. About 2-3 inch (blossom) across, trumpet shaped, the plant is up to 12 inches, average height. The sunlight is creeping back into the house—two or more weeks now since the summer solstice. Today, the clouds went away by 10 a.m. Will they stay away? Don's planning on it!

August 5: Well, I just tried to interfere with nature again—a baby rabbit was caught by a small weasel. The rabbit (snowshoe hare) tried to get away but had been injured enough so that the weasel caught it again. The rabbit was squealing so pitifully, I had to try to help the poor thing! But to no avail, unless I was willing to kill the weasel. They have to live, too!

August 20: Rain! Finally got almost one inch (.8) last night and yesterday. The clouds are coming and going. The clouds have been in and out of our area enough to keep Don from working outside much on his second painting in our yard this summer. Saw a moose in yard.

September 22: Goldfinches and hummingbirds. Hot temps in mid-80s. Heard birds the past two mornings: flycatchers, juncos, flickers, white-throated sparrows, warblers—all moving through. Migratory songbirds gone by mid-September.

October 6: We're parked on a hill on County Q in Dunn County, Wisconsin, near Knapp. The morning started out fine but by the time we got our breakfast and took off, the clouds were piled up in the west . . . Don had just put up his easel when it started to rain heavily. Back to the car. He sat and waited a few minutes and then set up again after it stopped storming. As for me, I'm reading and doing addresses on invitations to Don's show. I get out occasionally to restore circulation to my legs. I walk for a bit. It's fun to hear the birds, trees, and flora of my childhood and smell the wet ground. The smell is more rich [than the North Shore] because of more variety in growing and molding foliage. There's very little traffic on this road, making it fine for both of us. I get some privacy for times I need to use the "bathroom."

October 12: This is the most unusual of Don's setups to paint. He's parked on a county road, almost in the ditch, the tailgate up. He's sitting in the back end of the car, sort of sheltered from the rain. His umbrella is clamped to the tailgate for added protection. If the wind doesn't come up strong or a semi tears by he'll be able to paint! ... He's anxious to [keep] painting because this [Coon Valley, Wisconsin] is a most scenic area of valley farms, big trees, and bluffs. Great elements for paintings.

October 20: [Back in Silver Bay] The fall colors are still hanging on down on the shore. Makes me happy. Heard chickadees and saw juncos. Saw a huge flock of ravens fly southwest—about 200, I'd guess.

October 24: The temperature has hovered between 28 and 33 for three days. Saw a warbler today as it flew towards the kitchen window, then drop down and sit on the thermometer bracket. That's too late to be up here, I'd think. There are snow buntings flocking, and still some sparrows. Saw snow in the air off and on all week.

—◊—

BY THE END OF THE CENTURY the two Koestner children had traveled their own paths. Fred graduated from Hastings High School in 1981. Although a Merit Scholar finalist and salutatorian of his class of 400 students, he failed to get a college scholarship. Introverted and focused on getting good grades, he excelled in math and other sciences but avoided extracurricular activities. Ultimately, college screeners viewed him as less well-rounded than the student applicants they sought. Fred, certain that his top grades would bring him financial aid offers, was shocked and disappointed when none was offered.

That fall, with tuition money earned during the summer through his work for a Hastings paper products manufacturer, Fred enrolled in a two-year electronics program at Northwest Electronics Institute in Minneapolis. After graduation, he fixed copiers for six months, then got a job with an international electronics firm based in Edina, Minnesota. For the next eight years he traveled extensively as a service technician out of several field offices, first Harrisburg, Pennsylvania, then Munich, Germany, then San Jose, California. At first he fixed equipment. Later, tired of traveling and interested in settling down, he transferred to the company's Twin Cities headquarters.

In Minneapolis, Fred began dating a young woman he knew through his church, and they married in 1992. Dawn Johnson had completed college and law school and worked in a corporate legal department. She urged Fred to pursue the higher education he desired. Accepted into the engineering school at the University of Minnesota, Fred double-majored in geology and geological engineering while working part time. Upon graduating in 1995, he accepted a job with a Bloomington company specializing in environmental clean-up.

In 1998 Fred joined a fast-growing Eden Prairie-based firm as a software programmer. Fred's analytical mind, quiet manner, and knowledge of computer technology fit in well. A son, Benjamin, was born a few months into the new century; the family now lives in the Minneapolis suburb of St. Louis Park.

Lorna graduated from Hastings High School a year after Fred, in 1983, and like her brother was a Merit Scholar finalist and top student. Although "painfully shy," she pushed herself to broaden her interests in high school. She played in the band, helped with theater productions, and joined several activity clubs. She received a first-year full scholarship from Cornell College in Mount Vernon, Iowa, and graduated magna cum laude in 1986, with a double major in biology and philosophy. To pay off the student loans that allowed her to finish college, she trained in Seattle for a foreign-fisheries-observer program of the federal government, then worked several winters monitoring the catches of Korean trawlers operating in the Bering Sea. The next winter she monitored Japanese fishing boats in the Bering Sea and North Pacific.

In the spring of 1987 Lorna trained in Fairbanks, Alaska, as a volunteer botanist for the U.S. Fish and Wildlife Service and that summer camped on the tundra of the Arctic National Wildlife Refuge to conduct vegetation surveys. She was flown by helicopter every few weeks to new study sites. The next two summers she did similar work—as a paid employee, "camping and botanizing" on the coastal plain. Lorna also did a six-month stint at the refuge office in Fairbanks, and that winter studied Japanese. In April 1988 she attended a five-week conference in Japan at the farm of an organic farming expert who had lectured at Cornell.

In January 1991 Lorna returned to Japan, this time to board a Japanese research vessel for marine mammal surveys in the North Pacific, a joint research effort of the Japanese and U.S. governments. She spent nearly two months on the vessel as the sole U.S. researcher, returned to Japan, and then flew home. That spring she spent a month traveling in Central America, followed by three months apprenticing on an organic farm in Maine.

The following summer (1992) Lorna worked two months aboard the *Golden Alaska*, processing pollack into surimi, an imitation seafood popular in Japan. Though the messy job was less prestigious than observer work as a biologist, it paid better—enough that she could buy 70 acres of land near Carlton, south of Duluth. She had not stayed more than three months in any one place for the past six years and was tired of being a nomad. To finance her goal of settling on her property, she returned to the ocean for another season of processing fish.

The following spring and summer Lorna began construction of a log cabin from pines cut on her land. She bought a used tractor with a front-end loader to move the hefty logs into place. Friends, as well as her parents, helped with the building project. In August, she took another tour on the *Golden Alaska*. Between these two events she met Ed Fasula. They eventually married and have a son, Justin, born in 1996. Their marriage ended amicably in 2007. Lorna, the horticulturist for an environmental technologies group in northern Minnesota, plans to one day grow organic foods and cultivate native plants on her Carlton land.

Anyone who keeps the ability to see Beauty never grows old.
Franz Kafka

12

Split Rock Light

DON KOESTNER'S LONG, NARROW STUDIO was filled with paintings, some framed, many not. He carefully stacked the artwork vertically in a storage rack that rose to the ceiling. Another dozen or so paintings rested against the wall in two rows that were each six or seven paintings deep. On the walls were half a dozen others. An easel on each end of the room supported canvases he was working on. The basement was also filled with paintings.

"I'm painting myself into a corner," he said.

One day, his six-year-old grandson, Justin, looked around the crowded studio and asked, "If you have more paintings than you have room for, Grandpa, why do you keep painting more?"

"Because I like to," Grandpa replied.

In the fall of 2003, the Koestners were visited by painter friend Annette LeSueur. A graduate of Brigham Young University in Salt Lake City with a master's degree in fine arts, LeSueur later studied with Richard Lack for four years—she was the first female student accepted into his rigorous training program. Later, she started her own atelier in Minnetonka; she operated it successfully for more than 15 years. Now she teaches part time in her home and devotes much of her energy to publishing projects. She is an avid collector of late-nineteenth and early-twentieth-century children's books. The best and rarest of these are masterfully illustrated with pen-and-ink drawings and color engravings. She plans to include them in a children's art course she is developing to illustrate traditional drawing technique and composition.

Like Justin (Lorna's son), LeSueur was struck by Koestner's inventory and offered to take a dozen unsold paintings to the Twin Cities to find buyers. She was well connected with the traditional painting community of artists and patrons. She was also a voluble salesperson with a disarming manner.

Though Koestner valued her friendship and trusted her word, he didn't want to set himself up for disappointment. Still, he agreed to her taking the paintings. LeSueur loaded a dozen into her car, then called him a few weeks later: "Sold every one of them. I'll be back for more."

A fundamental characteristic of the marketplace is that few items change hands without a salesperson's nudge. Even people who claim to know what they like respond to assurances about value, price, and "taste." But many Minnesota art galleries provide only wall space, a promotional flyer and price list, maybe some cheese and wine. LeSueur hosted a series of three-hour open houses in the comfort of her book-lined apartment. Sometimes she allowed private showings. Those she invited were mostly people she knew as colleagues, students, or friends. Showing them a particular Koestner landscape, she pointed out its strengths and subtleties. Circling her index finger in front of a patch of milky sky, cascading water, or cluster of shimmering orange and yellow leaves, she might say, "Here is my favorite part of this painting," and explain how difficult it was for a painter to achieve. She talked knowledgeably about the soundness of Koestner's composition, his skillful use of color and value, his subtle brushwork. Next she discussed the painting in terms of the overall pleasure it delivered, then its investment value as a commodity in limited supply. Finally the clincher: They could buy an original Koestner without a gallery markup of 50 percent. To make the purchase possible to those who did not have several thousand dollars in the bank, she (with Koestner's approval) allowed a down payment with easy two-year terms and no-interest payments on the balance owed. Over the next several years, she made a dozen trips to Silver Bay, each time filling her Honda Civic "to the roof" with paintings to sell in her home. In all, she sold more than 200 paintings from the productive artist's inventory, for an amount totaling nearly $400,000—most of the revenue coming to Koestner in extended payments. From the start, LeSueur insisted on taking no commission on the sales.

Another Koestner supporter was painter Michael Coyle. A St. Cloud native, Coyle studied at the Minneapolis College of Art and Design and at the University of Minnesota for two years in the late 1970s, and later with Richard Lack. During the four years he was a Lack student, he supported himself by working nights as an aide in a group home for the developmentally disabled and by doing commercial art. Following that, he taught for several years at Atelier LeSueur while launching his painting career.

Coyle had long admired Koestner's work and visited his Silver Bay studio during summer painting trips to the North Shore. As

Koestner neared his 80th birthday in November 2003, Coyle was struck by the idea of producing an art book to commemorate Koestner's more than half a century of painting. The book would include photo reproductions of his paintings, a short biography, and some of the artist's technical notes. He discussed the idea with Annette LeSueur, and she agreed that the concept had merit. Don and Fern gave their consent to the project.

The ambitious undertaking involved locating as many original paintings as possible so that they could be professionally photographed and accurately reproduced in the book. Fern had kept a careful record of Don's painting sales over the years, and she contacted clients and patrons around the country for permission to photograph the Koestner paintings they owned. Most Minnesota clients and patrons she reached gave their consent. But those living out of state were reluctant to accept the risk of shipping their treasured paintings. Over the years, Fern had photographed many of the paintings herself, though most of the images were small 35mm slides that would not reproduce well when enlarged to a full-page size. Still, the three-year effort went forward and *Don Koestner: American Impressionist* was published in November 2005. Reproduced in full color were 135 Koestner paintings selected by Coyle and LeSueur from those they could obtain for the book, plus photographs of the artist at work. The ambitious publishing project involved dozens of volunteers, including Bill and Vicky Hakala, who edited the text and provided the biographical essay, final design, and production.

More than 300 people attended a gala book-signing at The Atelier Studio Program of Fine Art, a school operated by traditional painters and teachers Cyd Wicker and Dale Redpath on East Hennepin in Minneapolis. Most knew Koestner through past associations as patron, student, painting associate, and friend. They comprised a traditional art underground.

Mike Coyle's wife, Barbara, and several other volunteers provided an elaborate buffet for the weekend event. Don Koestner sat at a table for three hours signing books. He had pre-signed a hundred of them, hoping to free himself to visit with people during the show, but almost everyone who bought a signed book at the door got in line to have him personalize his copy. Some bought two or three copies to give to family members at Christmas. Several dozen Koestner landscapes were on display, and LeSueur worked the gallery floor to sell what she could. "I show no mercy," she teased. She sold every painting there.

LeSueur, who had known Koestner for nearly 30 years, could sell his work because she had a painter's understanding of the uniqueness of his talent, and respect for his integrity as a person and teacher. In the introduction she wrote for *Don Koestner: American Impressionist,* she described Koestner's visual memory: "He can glimpse the moment during a storm when the lighting is most dramatic or watch the subtle colors during a sunrise, hold them in his mind and then reproduce them on canvas with all the drama and power that were available to the rest of us only for a fleeting moment in time. He even seems to capture the temperature of the day."

—⁓—

ONE MAJOR CONTRIBUTOR to the book project was absent from the celebration. Fern Koestner died of lung cancer in May 2004, 18 months before the book was published. She would have basked in the glow of that event.

The cancer that preceded Fern's death first showed up only two months earlier. In bed one night in early March 2004, she had difficulty breathing and became panicky. Don called 911, and paramedics soon arrived to take her to the clinic in Two Harbors, 30 miles from Silver Bay. On the way, they administered oxygen to help her breathe and ease her anxiety. A scan at the clinic revealed a black spot on her left lung as well as some fluid collection. A doctor extracted the fluid with a needle inserted through the back of her rib cage. Further tests were done the next day at St. Lukes's Hospital in Duluth, and Fern returned home. Eleven days later she had a similar episode and a 911 call returned her to the Two Harbors clinic. With no motel rooms available that night, Don slept on a cot in her room. The medical staff again drew off the collected fluid and sent her home with a portable home-oxygen tank. A few days later, Lorna drove her mother to Duluth for a visit with the oncologist at St. Luke's. The prognosis was "not good." Fern's lung cancer was inoperable because of discovery too late to prevent its spread; chemotherapy would slow it down. She returned to the hospital a few weeks later for the first of several radiation treatments. She lost her appetite; most foods upset her stomach. Neighbors stepped in to cook for Don, including his Easter dinner.

In early May, Fern's sister, Beverly, agreed to move in with the Koestners for a few days to help out. During that time, she helped Fern come to terms with the reality of her condition and encouraged decisions on hospice care and a discussion of her funeral service—Fern's preferences. On Saturday, May 8, the night before Mother's Day, Fern suffered another episode of difficult breathing and ended up at St. Luke's. She died in her sleep three days later, on May 12, 2004—20 days before her 70th birthday. Don was devastated. He had never considered the possibility of Fern, thirteen years younger, ever being absent from his life. Only months before, they had planned a fall painting trip to Balltown, Iowa.

Fern had long been separated from the church of her youth, but she requested that her funeral be conducted by "The Faith," a group she had worshipped with before marrying Don. Fred and Lorna made most of the arrangements. The congregation's leader

led the service at a funeral chapel in Plymouth, a Minneapolis suburb. Gospels were read and hymns sung unaccompanied; 160 people signed the guestbook. The printed program included a poem
Fern wrote, one of 50 she self-published on the occasion of her
50th birthday in 1984. She titled the collection, *Fifty by Fifty by
Fern*. Following is "Haunted Shores":

> *The beach is empty, the sand*
> *where children ran is free*
> *of footprints. I see them*
> *still, shovels in hand,*
> *framing fantasies or*
> *throwing stones splashing*
> *into the lake.*
> *I hear their voices in washing*
> *waters and see their running*
> *in the small waves.*
> *The only continuity*
> *remains the changing lake.*

—◊—

ABOUT A YEAR BEFORE FERN DIED, Don developed a stomach dis-
order that caused him to lose 15 pounds over several months.
Because he was already thin at 125 pounds, the weight loss was
significant. Quoting Mark Twain, he said "I had no ballast to
throw over." Twain's observation was about the lack of vices to
give up in his old age. It also described Don Koestner. Thanks to
Fern, he ate simple, healthy foods. He didn't smoke or drink other
than an occasional bottle of beer. He was active, spent a lot of
time outdoors, and did work that he loved.

Because of his unusual stomach problems, Fern urged Don to
visit the Silver Bay Clinic. A resident doctor concluded that Don

had celiac sprue, a disease caused by the small intestine's inability to absorb nutrients. He recommended a nongluten diet and ordered a colonoscopy. Don lost another five pounds preparing and recovering from the colon exam and decided that the invasive procedure did him "more harm than good." He declined a follow-up test three years later.

Upon advice of the clinic dietitian, Don stopped eating store-bought breads made with gluten-rich wheat and barley flours and ate Fern's nongluten breads made with rice and potato flour, sorghum, and tapioca. To eliminate fat in his diet—another possible contributor to maldigestion, he switched from beef to grass-fed bison, an almost fat-free, antibiotic-free meat that he bought at Duluth's Whole Foods Co-op. Don and Fern bought other organically grown foods there. On his cereal he put rice milk instead of cow's milk. The new diet seemed to have good effect. He didn't regain lost weight but held the line. Following Fern's death, a blood test for celiac disease did not prove positive and Don found that his system could again tolerate many of the foods he had once enjoyed—some dropped off at his house by considerate neighbors.

Koestner's eyes troubled him increasingly during this period, a concern he worried about more than any other disability. Ten years earlier, in 1994, his optometrist had diagnosed macular degeneration in his left eye. For years, perhaps since birth, he also had astigmatism, one eye seeing higher than the other. Prisms in his glasses had kept his vision in balance, but now he required more correction than before. As he grew older, cataracts became another problem, and in 2004 his optometrist scheduled cataract surgery. On April 14, a month before Fern died, Don had his first operation. He said the surgery didn't improve his color perception but did allow him to see values better, "perhaps a shade lighter." To save his eyes for painting, Don took more frequent breaks and cut back on reading. For news and information, he listened to Wisconsin Public Radio.

For a quiet man, Koestner is emotionally intense. He has difficulty falling asleep at night unless he "unwinds" first by lying down, unoccupied, for a half hour or so. He takes a limited regimen of medication, some at bedtime, some at four-hour intervals through the day and night. Nevertheless, Koestner believes that "having a life that you love, and your health, does more to bring about longevity than medicines and doctoring."

Following Fern's death, Don experienced a solitariness that he hadn't known for 44 years. Fern filled his life with certainty and joy. She was ever present, ever supportive and sharing. From a practical standpoint, she also handled most of the details of their daily existence: planning and preparing meals, shopping, organizing, bookkeeping, correspondence. Don did routine home maintenance, tended the furnace, stacked wood, pumped lake water into the cistern every few weeks, and painted. After her death he said "I paint only a fourth of the time I used to."

—m—

WHEN PRESIDENT CLINTON SIGNED an IRS overhaul bill in July 1998, he energized an "open-space" preservation movement that in Minnesota spurred progress of the Minnesota Land Trust. The trust, formed seven years earlier, was aimed at protecting wild, scenic areas vulnerable to development. To participate in the program, an owner authorized a Land Trust easement on his or her property. The owner retained present use but agreed that his land would never be used for housing or commercial development or change in some other significant way. This restriction passes to any future owner when the property is sold. Present owners benefit from lower real estate taxes because the restrictions for resale reduce the site's value. The amount of decrease in value, shown by appraisals, is a gift to the Land Trust and therefore qualifies as a tax deduction. This benefit passes on to future owners.

Don and Fern had done little to disturb their natural setting in the 30 years they had owned the Silver Bay property, first as a summer retreat, then as a permanent home. But looking to the future, they wondered, when they died or became too frail to live there, what would become of the place? The North Shore had changed in three decades, upscale lodges replacing rustic vacation cabins and weathered cottages. Change had come slowly but with a feeling of inevitability. Here and there stands of birch and balsam had been cleared for souvenir shops and parking lots. On once solidly timbered hills on the north side of the lake, three-story homes with multiple lake-facing decks now declared themselves like June bugs splattered on a windshield. At neighboring Beaver Bay, town homes rose shoulder to shoulder above the rocky shoreline.

Although the Koestners stood to gain financially from the growing demand for real estate such as theirs, they had no intention of selling it for development. They felt they were stewards of the land and lake and in September 1998 eagerly signed up for the Minnesota Land Trust. The conservation easement stipulated that their home, set well back from the bluff and not visible from the lake, could be expanded by only 25 percent of its existing size.

The visiting field agent (using Fern's record of plant life) described the Koestner property on the date of her 1998 visit: "1.81 acres of Lake Superior shoreline, 35-to-45-foot cliffs, two small beaches, mixed forest of birch, spruce, balsam, pine. Other vegetation includes native orchids, coral roots, ladies' tresses, nodding trillium, wood anemone, aster, tansy, lupine, and fireweed. There is a narrow footpath down to a ladder leading down to one of the beaches. Except for the area adjacent to the house the property is undisturbed."

—⚋⚋—

IN THE FALL OF 2006, DON KOESTNER WAS INSPIRED to do a night painting of Lake Superior's century-old Split Rock Lighthouse—a North Shore icon. The lighthouse had guided freighters past its rocky shore since 1910 but stopped operating in 1969 following the adoption of electronic navigational aids. The Minnesota Historical Society, which manages the historic site, adopted the practice of briefly lighting the beacon several times a year—including November 10 (Veterans Day) to commemorate the sinking of the ore-carrier *Edmund Fitzgerald* in a November 1975 storm on the eastern end of the lake.

Koestner had painted Split Rock Lighthouse several times before, the most recent was in the summer of 2004, following Fern's death. His vantage point then was the shoreline some distance from the 130-foot cliff supporting the yellow brick tower. This time he would capture the light's reflection on the water from the same vantage point, but at night. In completing the earlier painting, he had counted roughly 140 steps to the painting site from the parking lot. This careful count allowed him, on repeated visits, to return to the same spot to set up his easel.

In the twilight of Veteran's Day 2006, Don recounted the steps —not to paint on location but to observe the light's reflection. He took the precaution of having company. A painter friend from Minneapolis, Wayne Howell and his wife, Pam, accompanied Don along the rock-strewn path to wait for complete darkness. The temperature was a comfortable 40 degrees F; there was a slight breeze, and they could hear a soft lapping of lake water against the rocky shore.

When they reached their spot on the shore, the beacon was already lit. Don was puzzled that the revolving light emitted a strong, yellow beam, yet there was no reflection whatever in the water. He became increasingly concerned, knowing such a reflection was necessary for his painting. Then, just before it became totally dark, the reflection suddenly appeared. Taking a few minutes to analyze its color and value, he mentally noted what he saw. The sky, overcast all evening, took on a dull purple glow, reflected in the lake. He said to himself, "Yellow and purple—a perfectly complementary color scheme!"

As always, the landscape's special mystery at first seemed impossible to capture with his small brush and palette of hand-ground paints. Still, he felt called to it. Don Koestner spent the winter months of 2006-07 painting the scene in the warmth of his studio. The challenge tested him, and the promise of spring gave him hope.

Acknowledgments

This biography greatly benefited from the trust and cooperation of the artist and his late wife, Fern Bolin Koestner. Much of the personal detail was derived from a series of recorded interviews with Don Koestner between 1992 and 94; earlier conversations, which began in the late 1960s, have continued into the present. Also helpful were Koestner's letters, journal notes and published writing, and reviews of his work. The artist's quest for new landscape subjects was described with the help of Fern's nature journals and diaries of painting trips—entries that also revealed her gift for observation, supportive spirit, and constant presence in her husband's life.

Other valuable sources include the Minnesota Historical Society research library, the James J. Hill Reference Library, and the library and archive of the Minneapolis School of Art. A centennial history of the Minneapolis Society of Fine Arts, *Their Splendid Legacy*, by Jeffrey A. Hess, provided background on the Minneapolis School of Fine Art's founding in 1886 and eventual shift in curriculum from rigorous "academic method" to training "artists for the future."

Cliff Moen, a Koestner colleague in the late 1940s, generously shared photographs and memories of road trips they took as art students, and a later bicycle tour of Europe. Cliff also provided a 1948 drawing of Koestner and several letters from him in 1956. Don Koestner's painting and teaching associate, Richard Lack, provided several photographs and stories of their long association. Artist Anna Quinn made available three dozen letters she and her husband, Brian, received from Koestner throughout the 1980s. In them, Koestner offered Anna encouragement in her painting, and sometimes described in detail his current projects. Also helpful were profiles of Koestner in local newspapers, and in selected issues of *Classical Realism Quarterly* published by the American Society of Classical Realism. The latter included a 1985 interview by editor Rebecca H. Anderson: "A Logical Path: an interview with plein-air master Don Koestner."

The Koestner children, Fred and Lorna, shared their experiences growing up in Nininger and on the North Shore. Fern's sister, Beverly Bolin Nelson, provided details on life in the Bolin household in the 1940s. Former Koestner neighbor and local historian Leslie Guelcher supplied background on the early history of Nininger. Peggy Yarborough explained the formation of the Heritage Art Gallery in Alexandria, Virginia. Richard Lack, Stephen Gjertson, and Annette LeSueur shared insights on Don Koestner's work.

A number of people agreed to critically read the text—a daunting commitment in their busy lives. The following provided editorial suggestions and technical corrections: Rich Cowles, Michael Coyle, Siri Hakala, Richard and Katherine Lack, Annette LeSueur, Christine Roen, and Paul Van Demark. All added body, texture, and accuracy to this story, and to all I am grateful.

I am hugely indebted to my wife, Vicky, for her partnership in bringing the story of this quiet and industrious artist onto the printed page. She not only read numerous drafts, but designed and produced *A Way of Living*. She has cherished this project as much as I.

Index

Photo pages numbered in italics.